Norway Travel Guide: Landscapes, Culture, and Beyond.

Kendrick Owens

All rights reserved. No part of this publication may be reproduced, distributed, or transmitted in any form or by any means, including photocopying, recording, or other electronic or mechanical methods, without the prior written permission of the publisher, except in the case of brief quotations embodied in critical reviews and certain other noncommercial uses permitted by copyright law.

Copyright © (KENDRICK OWENS) (2023).

TABLE OF CONTENTS

Introduction   9
Chapter 1. Norway   13
   1.1 About Norway   13
   1.2 Norway's Geography and Regions   16
   1.3 Norway's Climate and Best Time to Visit   19
   1.4 What to Wear   22
Chapter 2. Preparing for Your Trip   27
   2.1 Travel Documents and Visa Requirements   27
   2.2 Currency and Money Matters   30
   2.3 Packing Tips for All Seasons   33
   2.4 Travel Insurance and Health Precautions   36
Chapter 3. Transportation   41
   3.1 Getting to Norway   41
   3.2 Transportation within Norway   44
Chapter 4. Accommodation Options   49
   4.1 Hotels and Resorts   49
   4.2 Guesthouses and Bed & Breakfasts   52
   4.3 Hostels and Budget Accommodations   55
   4.4 Cabin Rentals and Camping Sites   58
   4.5 Family-Friendly Accommodation Suggestions   62
Chapter 5. Top Destinations in Norway   65
   5.1 Oslo   65
      5.1.1 Must-Visit Attractions   68
      5.1.2 Family-Friendly Activities   72
      5.1.3 Romantic Experiences for Couples   75
   5.2 Bergen   78
      5.2.1 Notable Landmarks and Sights   81

5.2.2 Activities for Kids ... 85
5.2.3 Romantic Spots for Couples ... 88
5.3 Tromsø ... 91
5.3.1 Northern Lights Viewing Points ... 94
5.3.2 Family-Friendly Arctic Adventures ... 97
5.3.3 Couples' Winter Escapes ... 100
5.4 Trondheim ... 103
5.4.1 Historical Sites and Museums ... 107
5.4.2 Family-Friendly Entertainment ... 110
5.4.3 Cozy Couple Activities ... 114
5.5 The Fjords ... 117
5.5.1 Exploring Norway's Fjords ... 121
5.5.2 Family-Friendly Fjord Tours ... 124
5.5.3 Romantic Fjord Cruises ... 127

Chapter 6. Family-Friendly Activities and Attractions ... **131**
6.1 Wildlife Parks and Zoos ... 131
6.2 Amusement Parks and Adventure Centers ... 134
6.3 Interactive Museums and Science Centers ... 137
6.4 Outdoor Recreation and Hiking for Families ... 140

Chapter 7. Romantic Experiences for Couples ... **145**
7.1 Secluded Getaways and Romantic Retreats ... 145
7.2 Romantic Cruises and Boat Tours ... 148
7.3 Candlelit Dinners with a View ... 151
7.4 Couples' Adventure Activities ... 154

Chapter 8. Norwegian Cuisine and Dining ... **159**
8.1 Traditional Norwegian Dishes to Try ... 159
8.2 Recommended Restaurants and Cafés ... 162
8.3 Vegetarian and Vegan Dining Options ... 165

8.4 Kid-Friendly Restaurants and Menus 169
Chapter 9. Cultural Experiences and Festivals 173
9.1 Norwegian Traditions and Customs 173
9.2 Folk Festivals and Celebrations 176
9.3 Art and Music Events 179
9.4 Cultural Activities Suitable for Families 183
Chapter 10. Outdoor Adventures and Nature Exploration 187
10.1 Hiking and Trekking Routes 187
10.2 Skiing and Snowboarding in Norway 190
10.3 Wildlife Safaris and Whale Watching 194
10.4 Camping and Outdoor Activities for Families 197
Chapter 11. Safety and Travel Tips 203
11.1 Emergency Numbers and Services 203
11.2 Safety Guidelines for Families 206
11.3 Responsible Travel and Environmental Awareness 209
Chapter 12. Language and Communication 215
12.1 Common Norwegian Phrases for Travelers 215
12.2 English Language Availability 217
Chapter 13. Traveling with Kids 221
13.1 Kid-Friendly Accommodations 221
13.2 Packing Essentials for Children 224
13.3 Childcare Services and Facilities 227
13.4 Tips for Keeping Kids Engaged During Travel 231
Chapter 14. Traveling as a Couple 235
14.1 Romantic Accommodations and Packages 235

    14.2 Couples' Activities and Itineraries   238
    14.3 Intimate Date Night Recommendations   241
Chapter 15. Traveling with Disabilities   **245**
    15.1 Accessibility Information and Resources   245
    15.2 Adaptive Tours and Activities   248
    15.3 Disability-Friendly Accommodations   252
Chapter 16. Itinerary Suggestions   **257**
    16.1 One Week Family Adventure   257
    16.2 Romantic Two-Week Getaway   260
    16.3 Multi-Generational Travel Experience   263
The Legend of the Northern Lights   **267**

Introduction

Welcome to the enchanting realm of Norway, a land of breathtaking fjords, majestic mountains, and vibrant cities that blend modernity with a deep-rooted appreciation for nature and culture. This comprehensive Norway travel guide is your passport to unlocking the wonders of this Nordic gem, catering to the diverse interests of every traveler, from families with kids to adventurous couples seeking romance in the wilderness.

Nestled in the northern reaches of Europe, Norway is a country that seamlessly weaves ancient traditions with contemporary innovations. Its stunning landscapes, ranging from the rugged Arctic wilderness in the north to the serene fjords and rolling hills in the south, have captured the imaginations of wanderers for centuries. Whether you're an avid explorer, a nature enthusiast, an art lover, or simply seeking a serene escape, Norway offers an array of experiences that will leave an indelible mark on your heart.

For families embarking on an unforgettable adventure with kids, Norway presents a wonderland of interactive museums, thrilling amusement parks, and wildlife encounters that will delight young minds. As you traverse the country, you'll find a welcoming culture that values family bonds and encourages exploration, making it an ideal destination for travelers of all ages.

Couples seeking to immerse themselves in romance will find Norway to be a dreamlike setting for intimate moments. From cozy cabins tucked away in the snow-capped mountains to charming cities offering candlelit dinners with a view, Norway sets the stage for captivating love stories amid some of the world's most awe-inspiring backdrops.

As you embark on this journey, we'll guide you through Norway's top destinations, sharing highlights, hidden gems, and the best activities for every type of traveler. Delve into the rich tapestry of Norwegian cuisine, from traditional delicacies to innovative culinary experiences. Witness the magic of local festivals and cultural celebrations that celebrate Norway's storied history.

In this guide, we'll equip you with essential travel tips, ensuring your safety and comfort throughout your stay. Whether you're curious about Norway's language and communication or seeking accessibility information for travelers with disabilities, we've got you covered.

Embrace the great outdoors with thrilling adventures, such as hiking through untouched wilderness, chasing the mesmerizing Northern Lights, or sailing across serene fjords. Or, take time to immerse yourself in Norway's vibrant cities, where cutting-edge architecture meets timeless heritage, and modern arts thrive alongside ancient traditions.

Norway is a land of contrasts and surprises, where every corner is a treasure trove waiting to be explored. So, pack your sense of wonder and an adventurous spirit, as we embark on an unforgettable journey through Norway's magnificent landscapes, cultural treasures, and warm-hearted communities. Let this guide be your companion, inspiring you to create memories that will last a lifetime in the land of the midnight sun and the dance of the Northern Lights. Welcome to Norway!

Chapter 1. Norway

1.1 About Norway

Norway, located in Northern Europe on the western part of the Scandinavian Peninsula, is a captivating and picturesque country that enchants visitors with its stunning natural landscapes, rich cultural heritage, and modern allure. Renowned for its fjords, mountains, and vibrant cities, Norway offers a diverse range of experiences that cater to travelers of all interests.

Nature's Majesty:
One of Norway's most iconic features is its awe-inspiring natural beauty. The country is famous for its deep, glacier-carved fjords that cut through the rugged coastline, providing a breathtaking backdrop for unforgettable boat cruises and hiking adventures. Majestic mountains, such as the towering peaks of the Jotunheimen and the snow-capped slopes of the Lyngen Alps, offer hikers and outdoor enthusiasts an opportunity to explore some of Europe's most pristine wilderness areas.

The Northern Lights, or Aurora Borealis, is a celestial spectacle that graces the Arctic skies of northern Norway. Witnessing the dance of colorful lights is a bucket-list experience, drawing visitors from around the globe during the winter months.

Modern Cities with Rich Heritage:
Norway's cities effortlessly blend contemporary living with historical charm. Oslo, the capital and largest city, is a vibrant hub of cultural attractions, modern architecture, and green spaces. It houses world-class museums, including the Viking Ship Museum and the Munch Museum, showcasing the works of renowned artist Edvard Munch.

Bergen, nestled between fjords and mountains on the western coast, is a UNESCO World Heritage City with a picturesque harbor, colorful wooden houses, and a lively fish market. Trondheim, in central Norway, boasts a rich history and impressive medieval architecture, including the iconic Nidaros Cathedral.

Outdoor Adventures:
For outdoor enthusiasts, Norway is a playground of activities. The country's extensive network of hiking trails caters to all levels, from leisurely strolls to challenging treks. During the winter, Norway transforms into a wonderland for skiers and snowboarders, offering world-class slopes and cross-country skiing opportunities.

Adventurous souls can explore Norway's wild side through activities like kayaking along the coast, spotting wildlife like whales and reindeer, and camping under the Midnight Sun during the summer months.

Warm and Welcoming Culture:
Norwegians are known for their friendly and inclusive nature, welcoming visitors with open arms. While the country embraces modern values, it also holds on to its deep-rooted traditions, including a strong connection to nature and a love for outdoor activities. Sami culture, indigenous to northern Norway, adds a unique layer of heritage to the country's identity.

Sustainability and Environmental Consciousness:
Norway takes great pride in its commitment to environmental sustainability. The country is a global leader in renewable energy, with a significant portion of its power generated from hydropower. Travelers will notice the widespread efforts to protect the environment, making it an ideal destination for eco-conscious tourists.

Whether you're seeking awe-inspiring natural beauty, immersive cultural experiences, thrilling adventures, or a combination of it all, Norway beckons with its distinctive charm. From the tranquil serenity of the fjords to the lively energy of its cities, Norway promises an unforgettable journey into the heart of Scandinavian allure.

1.2 Norway's Geography and Regions

Norway's geography is a captivating tapestry of diverse landscapes, showcasing a harmonious blend of majestic mountains, deep fjords, lush valleys, and expansive coastal stretches. Spanning from the rugged Arctic Circle in the north to the temperate climate of the southern coast, Norway offers a remarkable array of natural wonders that will leave travelers in awe.

1. Northern Norway:
The northernmost part of Norway is a region of untamed wilderness and Arctic beauty. Here, the land is dominated by dramatic fjords, towering mountains, and the vast expanse of the Arctic tundra. The iconic Lofoten Islands boast jagged peaks rising from the sea, while Tromsø, known as the "Gateway to the Arctic," offers exceptional opportunities to witness the Northern Lights during the winter months. Northern Norway is also home to the indigenous Sami people, known for their

distinctive culture, reindeer herding, and vibrant festivals.

2. Central Norway:
Central Norway is characterized by a striking landscape of steep mountains, deep valleys, and glacial lakes. The region is renowned for the majestic Jotunheimen National Park, which houses Norway's highest peaks, including Galdhøpiggen. Trondheim, Norway's third-largest city, is a historical gem with its impressive Nidaros Cathedral and charming old town.

3. Western Norway:
Western Norway is perhaps the most famous region, attracting visitors with its iconic fjords and picturesque coastal towns. The UNESCO-listed Nærøyfjord and Geirangerfjord are two of Norway's most breathtaking natural wonders, surrounded by steep cliffs and cascading waterfalls. The city of Bergen, a gateway to the fjords, exudes a charming atmosphere with its colorful wooden houses, bustling harbor, and vibrant cultural scene.

4. Eastern Norway:
Eastern Norway is the most populous and urbanized region, centered around the capital city, Oslo. This area offers a delightful mix of urban

pleasures and natural beauty. Oslo is a modern and cosmopolitan city, boasting world-class museums, green parks, and a waterfront teeming with life. Beyond the city, the region features serene lakes, rolling farmlands, and the charming villages of the Oslofjord.

5. Southern Norway:
The southernmost region of Norway offers a milder climate and a coastline adorned with sandy beaches and idyllic archipelagos. Kristiansand, a popular family destination, is known for its zoo and amusement park. The coastal town of Arendal entices visitors with its maritime charm, while Stavanger, located on the southwestern coast, is a gateway to the striking Preikestolen (Pulpit Rock) and Kjeragbolten.

6. Arctic Svalbard:
Located in the Arctic Ocean, Svalbard is an archipelago known for its polar landscapes, including glaciers, icebergs, and polar bears. Although technically a part of Norway, Svalbard has a distinct status with its own governance and unique travel regulations. The main settlement, Longyearbyen, serves as a starting point for Arctic adventures, including polar expeditions, wildlife

watching, and experiencing the polar day and polar night phenomena.

Each of Norway's regions has its own distinct charm, offering travelers a wealth of experiences, from exploring ancient cultural heritage to reveling in the untouched wilderness. Whether you're chasing the Northern Lights in the north or sailing through the awe-inspiring fjords in the west, Norway's geography promises a captivating journey through a land of natural splendor and cultural richness.

1.3 Norway's Climate and Best Time to Visit

Climate:
Norway's climate varies significantly throughout the country due to its long coastline and diverse geography. Generally, Norway experiences a temperate maritime climate influenced by the Gulf Stream, which moderates temperatures along the coast. Inland regions, especially in the northern areas, have a colder subarctic or Arctic climate.

Summer (June to August):
Summer is the most popular time to visit Norway, as the weather is relatively mild and the days are long. In Southern Norway, temperatures usually

range from 15°C to 25°C (59°F to 77°F), while the Northern regions may experience temperatures between 10°C to 20°C (50°F to 68°F). During this season, the landscapes are lush and vibrant, and outdoor activities such as hiking, sailing, and fishing are at their best. The Midnight Sun phenomenon occurs above the Arctic Circle, where the sun doesn't set, providing an enchanting experience for travelers.

Autumn (September to November):
Autumn is a beautiful time to visit Norway as the foliage changes colors, painting the landscapes with stunning hues. The temperatures gradually drop, especially in the north, and you may experience some rain. September is a great time for photography and hiking as the tourist crowds start to thin out.

Winter (December to February):
Winter in Norway is a magical time, particularly in the northern regions where you can witness the mesmerizing Northern Lights. Temperatures can be cold, ranging from -10°C to 5°C (14°F to 41°F) in the south and even colder in the north. However, this season offers fantastic opportunities for winter sports like skiing, snowboarding, and dog sledding. The southern coastal areas experience milder

winters, and cities like Bergen often have wetter and less snowy conditions.

Spring (March to May):
Spring is a transitional season, with temperatures slowly warming up and the snow melting. The landscapes come to life as flowers bloom, and nature awakens from its winter slumber. March and April are ideal months for skiing in the higher altitudes while enjoying milder temperatures in the lowlands. May is a beautiful time to visit as the days become longer, and outdoor activities become more accessible.

Best Time to Visit:
The best time to visit Norway depends on your preferences and the experiences you seek. Summer is ideal for exploring the fjords, hiking, and enjoying outdoor festivals. The Midnight Sun is a unique phenomenon to witness, especially in the Arctic regions.

Winter appeals to travelers looking for a winter wonderland experience, the Northern Lights, and winter sports enthusiasts. However, keep in mind that some remote areas may be less accessible during this time.

Shoulder seasons, such as late spring and early autumn, offer a balance between fewer tourists, pleasant weather, and various activities. During these times, you can enjoy both the last traces of winter activities and the vibrant beauty of spring or autumn landscapes.

Ultimately, the best time to visit Norway depends on your personal interests, whether it's experiencing the Arctic magic, enjoying the long summer days, or reveling in the beauty of autumn foliage. Regardless of the season, Norway's allure is ever-present, promising an unforgettable adventure in this land of captivating contrasts.

1.4 What to Wear

Norway's climate experiences distinct variations throughout the year, ranging from warm summers to cold winters, making it essential to pack appropriate clothing for each season. Here's a guide on what to wear for every season in Norway:

1. Spring (March to May):
Spring is a transitional season in Norway, with temperatures gradually warming up. However, it can still be chilly, especially in the early months. Packing layers is essential to adapt to changing

weather conditions. Consider including the following items in your spring wardrobe:

- Medium-weight Jacket: A waterproof and windproof jacket or a raincoat will protect you from occasional rain showers.

- Light Sweaters or Fleece: Wear these under your jacket for added warmth during cooler days.

- Long-Sleeve Shirts and T-shirts: These versatile pieces can be layered or worn independently, depending on the weather.

- Comfortable Pants: Opt for jeans, trousers, or lightweight hiking pants for outdoor activities.

- Comfortable Walking Shoes: Sturdy and waterproof shoes or hiking boots are suitable for exploring nature.

2. Summer (June to August):
Summer in Norway brings milder temperatures and longer days, making it an ideal time to explore the country's outdoors. While summers are generally pleasant, the weather can still be unpredictable, so be prepared with the following clothing:

- Lightweight Clothing: Pack T-shirts, shorts, skirts, and dresses for warmer days.

- Light Jacket or Sweater: Evenings can get cooler, so bring a light jacket or sweater to stay comfortable.

- Rain Gear: While summer is drier than other seasons, it's still wise to have a waterproof jacket or poncho on hand for any unexpected showers.

- Sun Protection: Bring a wide-brimmed hat, sunglasses, and sunscreen to shield yourself from the sun.

- Swimwear: If you plan to visit the coastal areas or take a dip in Norway's many lakes, pack your swimsuit.

3. Autumn (September to November):
Autumn in Norway is characterized by colorful foliage and cooler temperatures. As the season progresses, you'll experience cooler weather, so packing the right clothing is crucial:

- Medium-weight Jacket: A warm and waterproof jacket is essential as temperatures begin to drop.

- Layered Clothing: Pack sweaters, long-sleeve shirts, and light thermal wear to layer under your jacket.

- Comfortable Pants: Jeans or trousers are suitable for this season.

- Scarf and Gloves: As autumn progresses, the mornings and evenings can be chilly, so bring a scarf and gloves.

- Waterproof Shoes: Sturdy and waterproof footwear is essential for outdoor activities.

4. Winter (December to February):
Winter in Norway is cold, especially in the northern regions, where snow and freezing temperatures are common. To stay warm and comfortable, pack the following winter essentials:

- Heavy Winter Coat: A warm, insulated, and waterproof winter coat is a must.

- Thermal Layers: Wear thermal underwear and long-sleeve base layers to retain body heat.

- Wool Sweaters: Wool is an excellent insulator and keeps you warm even in damp conditions.

- Winter Accessories: Don't forget to bring a beanie, gloves, and a scarf to protect against the cold.

- Winter Boots: Insulated and waterproof boots with good traction are essential for walking on snow and ice.

- Snow Gear: If you plan to engage in winter sports, bring appropriate clothing such as snow pants and a snowsuit.

Regardless of the season, packing clothing that can be layered will allow you to adapt to changing weather conditions. Staying prepared with appropriate attire will ensure that you can fully enjoy your visit to Norway, no matter the time of year.

Chapter 2. Preparing for Your Trip

2.1 Travel Documents and Visa Requirements

Before embarking on your adventure to Norway, it is crucial to ensure you have all the necessary travel documents and meet the visa requirements for a smooth entry into the country. Here's a comprehensive overview of the essential documents you'll need:

1. Passport:
Ensure your passport is valid for at least six months beyond your planned departure date from Norway. This requirement applies to citizens of most countries, including the United States, Canada, the United Kingdom, Australia, and many others.

2. Visa Requirements:
Norway is a member of the Schengen Area, a group of 26 European countries that have abolished internal border controls. If you are a citizen of a country within the Schengen Area (e.g., EU countries), you do not need a visa to enter Norway for short stays of up to 90 days within a 180-day period. This also applies to citizens of certain non-EU countries, such as the United States, Canada, Australia, and New Zealand.

3. Visa-Free Travel:
For visa-free travel to Norway, you must hold a valid passport issued by an eligible country, and your visit should fall under the category of tourism, business, family visit, or transit. It is essential to note that you cannot work or study in Norway with a short-term visa exemption.

4. Long-Term Stay and Work Visas:
If you plan to stay in Norway for more than 90 days, work, study, or join family members who are residents in Norway, you will need to apply for a long-term visa or residence permit. Requirements for long-term visas vary depending on the purpose of your stay, and you should contact the Norwegian embassy or consulate in your home country for specific information and application procedures.

5. Schengen Visa:
For citizens of countries not included in the visa waiver program, you will need to apply for a Schengen Visa at the Norwegian embassy or consulate in your home country. The Schengen Visa allows you to travel to all Schengen countries, including Norway, for a short-stay visit.

6. Visa Application Process:

To apply for a visa or residence permit, you will need to submit a completed application form, a valid passport, passport-sized photos, proof of travel insurance, evidence of sufficient funds to cover your stay, and any specific documents related to the purpose of your visit (e.g., a letter of invitation, employment contract, or acceptance letter from an educational institution).

7. Travel Insurance:
It is highly recommended to have travel insurance that covers medical emergencies, trip cancellations, and other unforeseen events during your stay in Norway. Make sure the insurance is valid for the entire duration of your trip.

8. Travel with Children:
If you are traveling with children under the age of 18 and you are not their legal guardian, it is advisable to carry a notarized letter of consent from their parents or legal guardians, authorizing you to travel with them.

Remember that visa and entry requirements are subject to change, so it is essential to check the latest information on the official website of the Norwegian Directorate of Immigration (UDI) or consult the Norwegian embassy or consulate in your home country before you travel.

By ensuring you have the right travel documents and meet the visa requirements, you can focus on immersing yourself in the captivating beauty and experiences that Norway has to offer without any travel-related worries.

2.2 *Currency and Money Matters*

When traveling to Norway, it's essential to be familiar with the country's currency and money matters to ensure a smooth and hassle-free experience during your trip. Norway's currency is the Norwegian Krone, abbreviated as NOK, and it is denoted by the symbol "kr." Here are some important things to know about currency and managing your finances in Norway:

1. Currency Exchange:
   - The Norwegian Krone is the official currency used throughout the country. It is advisable to exchange your home currency for Norwegian Krone before your trip to avoid potential hassles upon arrival.
   - Currency exchange services are readily available at international airports, major train stations,

banks, and currency exchange offices in cities and popular tourist areas.
- It is recommended to compare exchange rates and fees at different locations to ensure you get the best value for your money.

2. Credit Cards and Debit Cards:
- Credit and debit cards are widely accepted in Norway, especially in urban areas and popular tourist destinations. Visa and Mastercard are the most commonly accepted cards, while American Express and other cards may have limited acceptance.
- Notify your bank before traveling to Norway to avoid any issues with your cards being blocked due to unusual international transactions.
- Automated Teller Machines (ATMs) are abundant in cities and towns, making it convenient to withdraw cash in Norwegian Krone using your debit card. However, do check with your bank regarding any foreign transaction fees.

3. Cash Usage:
- While credit cards are widely accepted, it's a good idea to carry some cash for smaller purchases or in case you visit more remote areas where card acceptance may be limited.

- In Norway, tipping is not mandatory, as a service charge is usually included in bills at restaurants and hotels. However, if you receive exceptional service, leaving a small tip is appreciated.

4. Budgeting and Expenses:
  - Norway is known for being a relatively expensive destination, so it's essential to plan and budget accordingly. Accommodation, dining, and transportation costs can add up quickly, but the experiences and natural beauty are well worth it.
  - To manage your expenses, consider exploring budget accommodation options, preparing some of your meals, and taking advantage of city passes or discount cards that offer savings on attractions and public transportation.

5. Value Added Tax (VAT) Refund:
  - Non-resident travelers may be eligible for a VAT refund on certain goods purchased in Norway. To claim the refund, make sure to ask for a tax-free shopping form from the retailer and present it at the customs office when leaving the country.

By being prepared and informed about currency and money matters in Norway, you can focus on enjoying your travel experiences without unnecessary financial stress. Embrace the beauty of the Norwegian landscapes, immerse yourself in the local culture, and savor every moment of your unforgettable journey in this enchanting Nordic nation.

2.3 Packing Tips for All Seasons

Norway's diverse climate and breathtaking landscapes make it a year-round destination, offering unique experiences in each season. However, due to its geographical variations, packing for a trip to Norway requires thoughtful consideration to ensure you're well-prepared for the weather conditions you may encounter. Whether you're traveling in the winter wonderland, the blooming spring, the vibrant summer, or the colorful autumn, here are essential packing tips for all seasons in Norway:

1. Layering is Key:
Regardless of the season, layering is essential in Norway. The weather can be unpredictable, with temperature fluctuations throughout the day. Pack a mix of lightweight and warm clothing, such as T-shirts, long-sleeved shirts, sweaters, and a versatile jacket or windbreaker. This way, you can easily adjust your clothing to stay comfortable in changing weather conditions.

2. Waterproof and Windproof Gear:
Norway's weather can be rainy and windy, especially along the coast and in the fjord regions. Be sure to pack a high-quality waterproof and windproof jacket and pants. These will not only keep you dry during rainy days but also provide an extra layer of protection against chilly winds.

3. Sturdy and Comfortable Footwear:
Bring sturdy and comfortable walking shoes or hiking boots suitable for various terrains. Norway's terrain can be uneven and rocky, so having proper footwear is crucial, especially if you plan on hiking or exploring the countryside.

4. Warm Clothing for Winter:
If you're traveling to Norway in winter, be prepared for cold temperatures, especially in the northern regions. Pack thermal underwear, insulated jackets, gloves, scarves, and a warm hat. Layering with wool or fleece materials is ideal for retaining body heat and staying cozy.

5. Pack Swimwear:
Don't forget to pack swimwear, even if you're visiting in winter. Many hotels and accommodations offer saunas and hot tubs, which are popular among Norwegians year-round.

Additionally, you might encounter hot springs or heated outdoor pools, providing a unique winter bathing experience.

6. Sun Protection for Summer:
Summers in Norway can be surprisingly warm, and the sun can be intense, especially in the northern regions. Bring sunglasses, a wide-brimmed hat, and sunscreen to protect yourself during long daylight hours.

7. Travel Adapter and Chargers:
Norway uses the Europlug Type C and Type F electrical outlets. Remember to bring a suitable travel adapter and chargers for your electronic devices.

8. Reusable Water Bottle:
Tap water in Norway is safe to drink and of excellent quality. Save money and reduce plastic waste by carrying a reusable water bottle to stay hydrated throughout your journey.

9. Insect Repellent (Summer):
In the summer months, especially in the northern regions, mosquitoes can be a nuisance. Pack insect repellent to protect yourself from bites during outdoor activities.

10. Camera and Binoculars:
Capture the stunning landscapes and wildlife encounters by bringing a camera with extra batteries and memory cards. Binoculars can also be handy for birdwatching and spotting wildlife.

By following these packing tips for all seasons, you'll be well-prepared to embrace the beauty of Norway and make the most of your unforgettable journey, no matter the time of year you choose to visit.

2.4 Travel Insurance and Health Precautions

Before embarking on your Norwegian adventure, it is essential to prioritize your well-being by obtaining comprehensive travel insurance and taking necessary health precautions. Norway is generally a safe and healthy country to visit, but being prepared for unexpected situations will provide peace of mind and ensure a smooth travel experience.

Travel Insurance:
Purchasing travel insurance is highly recommended for all travelers visiting Norway. A good travel insurance policy should cover medical emergencies,

trip cancellations or interruptions, lost baggage, and other unforeseen events that could disrupt your travel plans.

1. Medical Coverage: Ensure that your travel insurance includes medical expenses and emergency medical evacuation coverage. Norway has a high standard of medical care, but healthcare costs can be expensive for visitors. Having adequate medical coverage in your insurance policy will protect you from unexpected medical bills.

2. Trip Cancellation/Interruption: Life is unpredictable, and unforeseen circumstances may force you to cancel or cut short your trip. Trip cancellation/interruption coverage in your insurance will reimburse non-refundable expenses in such situations.

3. Baggage Loss/Delay: Travel insurance should also cover baggage loss, damage, or delay. In the unlikely event that your luggage is lost or delayed during your journey, this coverage will help compensate for essential items you may need to replace.

Health Precautions:

Norway has excellent healthcare facilities and a high standard of hygiene. However, it is still essential to take some health precautions to stay well during your trip.

1. Vaccinations: Check with your healthcare provider or a travel clinic about recommended vaccinations for Norway. Routine vaccinations such as measles, mumps, rubella, diphtheria, pertussis, and tetanus should be up to date. Depending on your travel history and specific plans, additional vaccines may be advisable.

2. Medical Kit: Carry a small medical kit with basic supplies like pain relievers, band-aids, antiseptic ointment, motion sickness medication, and any prescription medications you regularly take. While these items are readily available in Norway, having them on hand can be convenient, especially during outdoor activities.

3. Traveler's Diarrhea: Norwegian tap water is safe to drink, but if you plan on camping or hiking in remote areas, it's wise to bring water purification tablets or a portable water filter. Also, practice good hygiene and handwashing to reduce the risk of traveler's diarrhea.

4. Sun Protection: In summer, especially in the northern regions, the sun can be intense even when the weather seems cool. Bring sunscreen, sunglasses, and a hat to protect yourself from the sun's rays.

5. Insect Protection: While Norway doesn't have many disease-carrying insects, mosquitoes can be prevalent during the summer in certain areas. Bring insect repellent to ward off bites, particularly if you plan on spending time in forested or marshy regions.

By obtaining comprehensive travel insurance and taking necessary health precautions, you can focus on immersing yourself in the beauty of Norway without worries. Remember to stay informed about any travel advisories or health updates before your departure and always prioritize your well-being throughout your journey.

Chapter 3. Transportation

3.1 Getting to Norway

Getting to Norway is a seamless and enjoyable experience, thanks to its well-connected transportation network and numerous entry points. Whether you prefer air travel or an adventurous journey by land or sea, reaching this Nordic wonderland is convenient and efficient.

By Air:
Norway is served by several international airports, making it easily accessible from major cities worldwide. Oslo Gardermoen Airport, located just outside the capital city, is the country's primary gateway and handles numerous direct flights from major European and international destinations. Other key airports include Bergen Flesland Airport, Stavanger Sola Airport, and Trondheim Vaernes Airport, all of which offer international connections.

Travelers from North America, Asia, and other distant locations can find convenient flight options with major airlines that connect through major European hubs. Flight durations may vary depending on the departure city, with direct flights from Europe generally taking a few hours, while journeys from more distant locations may involve longer travel times.

By Sea:
If you prefer a scenic approach to Norway, arriving by sea is a wonderful option. Cruise ships regularly call at Norwegian ports, allowing travelers to embark on a majestic journey through the country's iconic fjords. Ports like Bergen and Oslo are popular stops for many cruise lines offering a range of itineraries, catering to different preferences and budgets.

Ferry services also operate between Norway and neighboring countries, such as Denmark, Sweden, and Germany, providing a delightful and relaxed way to travel, especially for those traveling with vehicles or seeking a unique coastal experience.

By Land:
Norway shares land borders with Sweden, Finland, and Russia (via the far northeastern region), making overland travel a possibility for visitors from neighboring countries. Scandinavia is well-connected by road networks, allowing for easy cross-border travel via car, bus, or train.

Trains, in particular, offer comfortable and scenic journeys to Norway. The "Norway in a Nutshell" tour is a popular route, combining train rides with boat cruises through the fjords, showcasing some of Norway's most picturesque landscapes.

Travel within Norway:
Once in Norway, traveling within the country is a breeze. An efficient and reliable public transportation system, including trains, buses, and ferries, connects major cities and towns. The scenic train routes, such as the Bergen Line and the Flam Railway, offer unforgettable journeys through Norway's diverse landscapes.

For those seeking more flexibility and off-the-beaten-path exploration, renting a car or a campervan is an excellent option. Norway's well-maintained roads make self-driving a pleasure, enabling travelers to venture into remote areas and discover hidden gems at their own pace.

Traveling by air within Norway is also an option, with domestic flights connecting major cities and remote regions. It's worth considering domestic flights for longer distances, such as between Oslo and Tromsø or Bergen and Kirkenes, to save time and cover vast distances quickly.

As you embark on your journey to Norway, rest assured that the country's transportation infrastructure is designed to ensure a seamless and enjoyable travel experience. Whether you're arriving by air, sea, or land, or exploring within the country, Norway's well-connected networks will enhance your adventure and set the stage for unforgettable memories in this mesmerizing Nordic paradise.

3.2 Transportation within Norway

Norway's efficient and well-connected transportation system makes exploring the country a breeze, whether you're navigating the vibrant cities or venturing into the remote wilderness. From modern trains and buses to scenic ferries and domestic flights, travelers have a variety of options to choose from, ensuring smooth and comfortable journeys throughout their Norwegian adventure.

1. Trains:
Norway boasts an extensive and reliable railway network, operated by Vy (formerly known as NSB). The trains are known for their punctuality and comfortable amenities, making train travel an excellent option for getting between major cities and regions. The Oslo-Bergen Railway, often

referred to as one of the most beautiful train rides in the world, offers breathtaking views of the scenic countryside and fjords during its journey.

2. Buses:
Buses are a convenient and cost-effective way to travel within Norway, especially to destinations not accessible by train. Nor-Way Bussekspress and other regional bus companies provide intercity and regional services, connecting smaller towns and remote areas. The buses are modern, equipped with free Wi-Fi, and offer a comfortable travel experience.

3. Ferries:
With its extensive coastline and numerous islands, ferries play a crucial role in Norway's transportation system. Ferry rides offer an opportunity to witness the stunning fjords up close and enjoy the picturesque coastal scenery. Ferries operate on several routes, including the popular ones like the Geirangerfjord and the Hurtigruten coastal voyage, which takes you along the Norwegian coast from Bergen to Kirkenes.

4. Domestic Flights:
For travelers covering longer distances or wanting to reach northern regions quickly, domestic flights

are a viable option. Avinor operates several airports across Norway, connecting major cities and towns. Airlines like SAS and Norwegian Air Shuttle provide domestic flight services, offering convenient connections between regions.

5. Car Rentals and Campervans:
Renting a car or a campervan is an excellent way to explore Norway at your own pace, especially if you want to venture off the beaten path. The well-maintained road network allows for comfortable road trips, and it's a great option for families or couples seeking flexibility in their itinerary. However, if traveling during winter, be prepared for potential weather challenges and road conditions in certain regions.

6. City Transport:
Major cities like Oslo, Bergen, Trondheim, and Stavanger have efficient public transportation systems, including buses, trams, and metros. Oslo, for instance, offers an extensive metro network, making it easy to get around and visit popular attractions. Travelers can purchase travel cards for convenience and cost savings while exploring the cities.

7. Cycling:

Norway's cycling culture is strong, and many cities have dedicated cycling lanes, making it a bike-friendly destination. Renting bikes or joining cycling tours is a fantastic way to experience the beautiful landscapes and explore the cities from a different perspective.

8. Accessibility:
Norway places great emphasis on accessibility for all travelers, including those with mobility challenges. Most public transportation facilities and major tourist attractions are equipped with facilities to accommodate people with disabilities.

Whether you prefer the scenic routes of trains and ferries or the freedom of a road trip, Norway's transportation options ensure that your travel within the country is seamless and enjoyable. Plan your itinerary wisely, taking into account the distances and modes of transportation available, and get ready to embark on an unforgettable journey through Norway's picturesque landscapes and captivating cities.

Chapter 4. Accommodation Options

4.1 Hotels and Resorts

When it comes to accommodations in Norway, travelers are spoiled for choice with a range of options that cater to every taste and budget. From boutique hotels with stunning fjord views to cozy mountain lodges immersed in nature, Norway's lodging options ensure a comfortable and memorable stay.

1. Fjord-Facing Hotels:
For an unforgettable experience, consider staying in a hotel or resort overlooking Norway's breathtaking fjords. Imagine waking up to panoramic views of the serene waters and majestic cliffs. Many fjord-facing properties offer spacious balconies or outdoor terraces, allowing guests to savor the natural beauty right from the comfort of their rooms.

Suggested Hotel: Hotel Ullensvang in Lofthus. Nestled on the shores of the Hardangerfjord, this family-run hotel boasts lush gardens, an indoor and outdoor pool, and a private beach. It's an ideal base for exploring the surrounding orchards and waterfalls.

2. City Chic Hotels:
Norway's vibrant cities are home to an array of stylish and modern hotels that cater to urban explorers. These hotels often combine contemporary design with convenient locations near cultural attractions, shopping districts, and bustling restaurants.

Suggested Hotel: The Thief in Oslo. This luxurious waterfront hotel not only offers elegant rooms with stunning views of the Oslofjord but also features an impressive art collection throughout the property, making it an artistic haven in the heart of the city.

3. Mountain Retreats and Ski Resorts:
For travelers seeking a winter wonderland or a tranquil escape in nature, Norway's mountain resorts and lodges deliver an idyllic retreat. During the winter months, many of these resorts provide easy access to ski slopes and snow-covered landscapes, while summer brings opportunities for hiking and other outdoor activities.

Suggested Resort: Norefjell Ski & Spa in Noresund. Situated just a couple of hours from Oslo, this luxurious ski resort offers a wide range of activities, including skiing, spa treatments, and hiking. Its modern alpine-style architecture blends perfectly with the surrounding nature.

4. Unique and Quirky Stays:
For those looking to step away from the ordinary, Norway offers a variety of unique accommodations that promise an unforgettable experience. Stay in a traditional Sami tent called a "lavvu" and immerse yourself in Sami culture, or book a stay at an ice hotel during the winter months.

Suggested Experience: Sorrisniva Igloo Hotel in Alta. Constructed entirely from ice and snow each year, this hotel offers a magical icy escape during the winter season. With beautifully carved ice sculptures and cozy sleeping bags, guests can enjoy a true Arctic adventure.

5. Coastal and Island Retreats:
Norway's coastline is peppered with charming coastal towns and serene islands, and there are plenty of hotels and resorts that capitalize on these scenic locations. Relax by the seaside, indulge in fresh seafood, and take in the tranquility of the Norwegian coast.

Suggested Hotel: Reine Rorbuer in Lofoten. Offering traditional fishermen's cabins set against a dramatic backdrop of mountains and sea, this resort captures the essence of Norway's coastal charm. Visitors can also engage in activities like fishing and kayaking.

No matter where your travels take you in Norway, rest assured that a wide array of accommodation options awaits, each offering its unique charm and hospitality. From luxurious hotels with fjord views to rustic mountain lodges and quirky stays, Norway's hotels and resorts are sure to enhance your overall travel experience.

4.2 Guesthouses and Bed & Breakfasts

For travelers seeking a more intimate and cozy accommodation experience, Norway offers a delightful array of guesthouses and bed & breakfasts (B&Bs). These charming establishments provide a warm and welcoming ambiance, often run by hospitable hosts who take great pride in sharing their local knowledge and culture with guests. Staying at a guesthouse or B&B not only offers a comfortable place to rest but also an opportunity to immerse yourself in the authentic Norwegian lifestyle.

Characteristics of Guesthouses and Bed & Breakfasts:

Norwegian guesthouses and B&Bs are typically found in picturesque locations, nestled amidst nature, and offer a personal touch that larger hotels may lack. Many of them are converted farmhouses, cottages, or historic buildings, which adds a unique charm to your stay. You can expect cozy rooms adorned with traditional decor and modern amenities, making you feel right at home.

In the morning, wake up to the aroma of freshly brewed coffee and indulge in a hearty Norwegian breakfast, often featuring locally sourced ingredients like artisanal cheeses, homemade jams, and freshly baked bread. The hosts' genuine hospitality and personalized attention create a warm atmosphere, making your stay memorable.

Suggested Guesthouses and Bed & Breakfasts:
1. Tranquil Fjord Retreat (Geirangerfjord): Nestled on the banks of the awe-inspiring Geirangerfjord, this family-run guesthouse offers captivating views of the UNESCO World Heritage-listed fjord. Relax in comfortable rooms with panoramic windows, allowing you to soak in the majestic scenery from the comfort of your bed. The hosts are delighted to arrange fjord cruises and outdoor activities, ensuring an unforgettable experience in Norway's fjord country.

2. Coastal Charmer (Lofoten Islands):
Set in the heart of the stunning Lofoten archipelago, this traditional B&B offers a true taste of coastal Norway. Wake up to the sound of seagulls and the gentle lapping of waves, as you stay in charming fisherman's cabins. The hosts, local fishermen themselves, share captivating tales of life on the rugged coast. Take part in fishing excursions, hike along the dramatic cliffs, and feast on freshly caught seafood prepared by the hosts.

3. Historic Mountain Lodge (Jotunheimen National Park):
Immerse yourself in the splendor of Norway's highest mountains at this historic mountain lodge, dating back to the 19th century. Located in the heart of Jotunheimen National Park, this guesthouse offers a cozy retreat after a day of hiking and exploring the wilderness. Gather around a crackling fireplace in the evenings and enjoy traditional Norwegian dishes prepared with love by the lodge's chef.

4. Secluded Wilderness Getaway (Tromsø):
Escape to this remote wilderness B&B, situated on a secluded island off Tromsø's coast. Accessible only by boat, this tranquil retreat offers an ideal spot for

Northern Lights viewing during the winter months. Experience the serenity of Arctic nature, engage in ice fishing, and warm up in a traditional wood-fired sauna. The hosts, Arctic enthusiasts and seasoned aurora hunters, share their knowledge of the Northern Lights, ensuring an unforgettable Arctic adventure.

When seeking an authentic and intimate experience in Norway, consider staying at one of these delightful guesthouses or B&Bs. You'll not only create lasting memories but also forge connections with locals who share their love for Norway, leaving you with a deeper appreciation for the country's natural wonders and cultural heritage.

4.3 Hostels and Budget Accommodations

Traveling to Norway doesn't have to break the bank, as the country offers a range of hostels and budget accommodations that provide comfortable stays without compromising on memorable experiences. Embracing the spirit of camaraderie and affordability, these budget-friendly options present an excellent opportunity to connect with fellow travelers while exploring the wonders of Norway.

Hostels:

Hostels in Norway are known for their laid-back atmosphere, communal spaces, and opportunities to meet like-minded travelers from around the world. They are especially popular among backpackers, solo adventurers, and young travelers seeking affordable and social accommodation options.

Most hostels in Norway provide shared dormitory-style rooms with bunk beds, as well as private rooms for those looking for a bit more privacy. Common areas, such as lounges, kitchens, and outdoor spaces, encourage interaction and provide spaces to unwind after a day of exploration.

Budget Accommodations:
In addition to hostels, budget-conscious travelers can find other affordable lodging options, including guesthouses, budget hotels, and even some campgrounds with basic cabins or cottages for rent. These accommodations often provide essential amenities, such as Wi-Fi, comfortable beds, and shared facilities, making them ideal for travelers who prefer simplicity and value.

Suggested Budget Accommodations in Norway:

1. Anker Hostel (Oslo):

Located in the heart of Oslo, Anker Hostel is a popular choice for travelers seeking a budget-friendly stay in the Norwegian capital. With a variety of room types, including private rooms and shared dormitories, this hostel offers comfortable accommodation at reasonable rates. The hostel also provides a communal kitchen, a lively bar, and easy access to public transportation, making it an excellent base for exploring Oslo's attractions.

2. Bergen YMCA Hostel:
Situated in the charming city of Bergen, the Bergen YMCA Hostel is a cozy and welcoming option for budget travelers. Its convenient location allows easy access to Bergen's famous Bryggen Wharf and other attractions. The hostel offers both private rooms and dormitories, and guests can enjoy facilities like a communal kitchen and a comfortable lounge area with panoramic views of the city.

3. Rorbu (Lofoten Islands):
For a unique and budget-friendly experience in Norway's picturesque Lofoten Islands, consider staying in a traditional rorbu, a cozy fishing cabin. Many rorbuer have been converted into affordable self-catering accommodations, providing an

authentic and rustic stay amid stunning coastal landscapes.

4. Citybox Oslo:
Citybox Oslo offers minimalist and stylish budget accommodations in the heart of Oslo's city center. Embracing the concept of no-frills comfort, this hotel provides self-check-in kiosks, allowing guests to manage their stay independently. With affordable room rates and a central location, Citybox Oslo is an excellent option for budget-conscious travelers who prefer a more hotel-like experience.

When exploring Norway on a budget, these hostels and budget accommodations offer a fantastic blend of affordability, convenience, and opportunities to connect with fellow travelers. Embrace the spirit of adventure and make unforgettable memories without compromising your travel budget!

4.4 Cabin Rentals and Camping Sites

For travelers seeking an authentic and immersive experience in Norway's stunning natural landscapes, cabin rentals and camping sites are the perfect choices. Norway's vast wilderness and abundant national parks provide a plethora of opportunities for outdoor enthusiasts to connect with nature and create lasting memories.

Cabin Rentals: Embrace Cozy Retreats Amidst Nature

1. Fjordside Cabins:
Nestled along the picturesque fjords, these cozy cabins offer unparalleled views of the shimmering water and towering cliffs. Wake up to the sound of gentle waves and breathe in the crisp, clean air right from your doorstep.

2. Mountain Retreats:
Escape to remote mountainous regions and stay in rustic mountain cabins. Surrounded by breathtaking peaks and lush meadows, these accommodations provide a serene escape for hikers and nature lovers.

3. Arctic Cabins:
For an extraordinary adventure, head to the Arctic regions of Norway and stay in cabins offering front-row seats to the enchanting Northern Lights. Witness the celestial display from the warmth and comfort of your cabin.

Camping Sites: Embrace the Freedom of the Great Outdoors

1. National Park Camping:
   Norway boasts a network of well-maintained camping grounds within its national parks. Set up your tent amidst lush forests, near serene lakes, or along winding trails, and immerse yourself in the untouched beauty of nature.

2. Fjord Camping:
   Experience the essence of Norway by camping alongside the fjords. Enjoy unparalleled sunsets, kayaking opportunities, and a chance to witness the elusive Midnight Sun during the summer.

3. Island Camping:
   Venture to Norway's numerous coastal islands and camp on pristine shores. Connect with the tranquility of the sea, and perhaps try your hand at fishing or crabbing for a memorable experience.

Tips for Cabin Rentals and Camping:

1. Booking in Advance: Cabin rentals, especially in popular areas, can get fully booked quickly, so it's advisable to make reservations well in advance, especially during peak travel seasons.

2. Pack Accordingly: While cabins provide basic amenities, camping requires more preparation. Pack appropriate gear, including a sturdy tent, sleeping bags, and warm clothing, to ensure a comfortable stay.

3. Leave No Trace: Norway's commitment to environmental sustainability extends to its outdoors. Always follow the principles of "Leave No Trace" camping to preserve the pristine beauty of nature for future generations.

4. Safety First: Prioritize safety during outdoor adventures. Inform someone about your travel plans, be aware of weather conditions, and follow guidelines for camping in designated areas.

Cabin rentals and camping sites in Norway offer the chance to disconnect from the hustle and bustle of everyday life and reconnect with the beauty of the natural world. Whether you choose a fjordside cabin for a romantic escape or opt for camping beneath the Midnight Sun with friends, these experiences will undoubtedly leave you with a deep appreciation for Norway's unparalleled wilderness.

4.5 Family-Friendly Accommodation Suggestions

Norway, with its family-oriented culture and captivating landscapes, offers a plethora of family-friendly accommodations that cater to the needs of travelers with children. From cozy cabins in the mountains to charming hotels by the fjords, families are sure to find comfort and convenience during their stay in this enchanting country.

1. Family-Friendly Hotels:
   Many hotels throughout Norway are well-equipped to accommodate families, offering spacious rooms and amenities suitable for children. Look for hotels with family rooms or suites that have extra beds or connecting rooms to ensure everyone has their space. Some hotels also provide play areas, babysitting services, and kid-friendly activities to keep the little ones entertained.

   Example Hotel: Family Haven Oslo - Located in Oslo, Family Haven Oslo is renowned for its family-friendly ambiance. With spacious suites, a dedicated play area, and proximity to major attractions, it's an ideal choice for families exploring the Norwegian capital.

2. Cabin Rentals:

Embrace the charm of Norwegian wilderness by renting a cozy cabin amidst the mountains or by a serene lake. Cabin rentals provide families with the freedom to cook their meals, enjoy the privacy of their own space, and immerse themselves in nature. Many cabin accommodations offer outdoor playgrounds and barbecue facilities, adding to the overall family experience.

Example Cabin: Fjord View Log Cabins - Situated in the heart of the fjords, Fjordview Log Cabins provide families with stunning views, fully equipped kitchens, and outdoor play areas. It's the perfect spot for families seeking a tranquil retreat with a touch of adventure.

3. Farm Stays:
For a unique and immersive experience, consider staying at a traditional Norwegian farm. Farm stays offer families the chance to interact with animals, participate in farm activities, and experience authentic rural life. Kids will love feeding the animals, milking cows, and exploring the picturesque countryside.

Example Farm Stay: Family Farm Adventures - This family-run farm in the Norwegian countryside offers cozy accommodations, farm tours, and hands-on activities for kids. It's an excellent choice for families looking to connect with nature and learn about farming.

4. Resorts with Family Facilities:
   Family-friendly resorts in Norway often feature an array of amenities tailored to children, such as swimming pools, indoor play areas, and organized activities. Some resorts even offer childcare services, allowing parents to enjoy some leisure time while knowing their kids are in good hands.

   Example Resort: Fjordland Family Resort - Nestled in a picturesque fjord setting, Fjordland Family Resort offers spacious family suites, a kids' club, and a range of outdoor activities for all ages. It's an excellent base for exploring the nearby fjords and enjoying quality family time.

Remember to book your family-friendly accommodation well in advance, especially during peak travel seasons, to ensure a stress-free and enjoyable stay in Norway. The country's family-focused hospitality ensures that both parents and children will have a memorable experience as they explore the wonders of Norway together.

Chapter 5. Top Destinations in Norway

5.1 Oslo

As the capital and largest city of Norway, Oslo stands proudly at the forefront of Scandinavian charm, effortlessly blending a rich cultural heritage with modern sophistication. Nestled amidst stunning natural landscapes, Oslo offers a unique fusion of cosmopolitan city life and the tranquil embrace of nature, making it a must-visit destination for travelers seeking a diverse and enriching experience.

Cultural Treasures and Museums:
Oslo boasts a wealth of cultural treasures that showcase the country's fascinating history and artistic achievements. History enthusiasts can explore the Viking Ship Museum, where remarkably preserved Viking ships reveal the seafaring prowess of ancient Norse civilization. The Fram Museum offers a glimpse into the intrepid world of polar exploration, housing the legendary Fram ship used by Roald Amundsen in his Arctic expeditions.

Art lovers will find their passions ignited at the Munch Museum, dedicated to the works of Norway's iconic artist, Edvard Munch. Witness masterpieces like "The Scream" and "The

Madonna," which have left an indelible mark on the art world. For contemporary art, the Astrup Fearnley Museum showcases cutting-edge exhibits and a remarkable collection of contemporary pieces.

Historic Landmarks and Architecture:
Stroll through Oslo's streets, and you'll encounter an intriguing blend of architectural styles, ranging from historic gems to modern masterpieces. The Royal Palace, a grand neoclassical structure, stands elegantly in the heart of the city and serves as the official residence of the Norwegian Royal Family.

The Akershus Fortress, a medieval castle overlooking Oslo's harbor, tells tales of the city's past, while the striking Oslo Opera House, with its striking marble and glass exterior, represents contemporary architectural brilliance. Be sure to visit the iconic Holmenkollen Ski Jump, offering panoramic views of Oslo and a glimpse into the city's passion for winter sports.

Nature in the City:
Nature seamlessly intertwines with urban life in Oslo, allowing visitors to enjoy the best of both worlds. The city is dotted with lush parks and green spaces, providing ample opportunities for

relaxation and outdoor activities. The Vigeland Park, a world-renowned sculpture park, captivates with over 200 impressive sculptures by artist Gustav Vigeland, celebrating the human experience.

Bygdøy Peninsula, just a short ferry ride away, beckons with its museums, beaches, and forests, making it an ideal retreat for nature lovers. Wander along the waterfront promenades of Aker Brygge and Tjuvholmen, offering stunning views of the Oslo Fjord and a lively atmosphere with charming cafés, restaurants, and boutique shops.

Culinary Delights:
Oslo's dining scene is a gastronomic delight, with a focus on fresh, locally sourced ingredients and innovative culinary concepts. Embrace the city's love for seafood with a visit to the famous Fish Market, where you can savor an array of delectable dishes straight from the sea.

For a taste of traditional Norwegian cuisine, try "rømmegrøt" (sour cream porridge) or the beloved "smørbrød" (open-faced sandwiches) at local eateries. Don't forget to indulge in the delightful Norwegian pastries, such as "kanelboller" (cinnamon buns) and "Skillingsbolle" (cardamom-flavored buns) at cozy bakeries.

Welcoming Atmosphere:
Oslo's friendly and welcoming atmosphere adds an extra layer of allure to the city. Locals take pride in their city's cultural offerings, and many are fluent in English, making it easy for visitors to communicate and connect with the vibrant community.

With its captivating blend of art, history, nature, and cuisine, Oslo invites travelers to immerse themselves in the heart of Norwegian culture. Whether you're exploring its renowned museums, gazing at architectural wonders, or simply savoring the tranquility of its parks, Oslo is a city that promises an unforgettable adventure at every turn.

5.1.1 Must-Visit Attractions

Oslo, the vibrant capital of Norway, is a city that seamlessly blends modern sophistication with a deep appreciation for nature and culture. As you explore this Scandinavian gem, you'll discover a plethora of attractions that cater to a diverse range of interests. From world-class museums and historic landmarks to serene parks and architectural wonders, Oslo has something to captivate every traveler. Here are some must-visit attractions to include in your itinerary:

1. Viking Ship Museum:
Immerse yourself in the rich Viking history at the Viking Ship Museum, located on the Bygdøy Peninsula. The museum houses exceptionally preserved Viking ships, including the Oseberg, Gokstad, and Tune ships, along with an array of artifacts and exhibits that offer insights into Norway's seafaring past.

2. Vigeland Park (Frogner Park):
A true masterpiece of sculpture and design, Vigeland Park is the largest sculpture park in the world by a single artist, Gustav Vigeland. Stroll through the beautifully landscaped gardens to admire over 200 bronze and granite sculptures that depict the human experience in various forms and emotions.

3. The Royal Palace (Det kongelige slott):
Located at the end of Oslo's main street, Karl Johans gate, the Royal Palace is the official residence of the Norwegian monarch. Visitors can witness the daily changing of the guard and, during the summer, explore the palace's stunning interiors and lush gardens.

4. The Munch Museum:

Art enthusiasts should not miss a visit to the Munch Museum, dedicated to the life and works of the renowned Norwegian artist, Edvard Munch. The museum houses an extensive collection of Munch's paintings, drawings, prints, and sculptures, including his most famous work, "The Scream."

5. The Fram Museum:
Explore the fascinating history of polar exploration at the Fram Museum. Here, you can step aboard the Fram, the world's strongest wooden ship, which carried explorers Fridtjof Nansen and Roald Amundsen on their expeditions to the Arctic and Antarctic regions.

6. The Opera House (Operahuset):
An architectural marvel, the Oslo Opera House is an iconic landmark on the waterfront. Its striking design allows visitors to walk on its sloping roof, providing panoramic views of the city and the Oslofjord.

7. Akershus Fortress (Akershus festning):
Dating back to the 13th century, Akershus Fortress is a historic castle and fortress that has played a crucial role in Oslo's history. Explore its medieval halls, defensive walls, and enjoy beautiful views of the harbor.

8. Holmenkollen Ski Jump and Museum:
For sports enthusiasts, a visit to the Holmenkollen Ski Jump and Museum is a must. Admire the impressive ski jump structure, which offers panoramic views of Oslo, and learn about the history of skiing and winter sports in Norway.

9. National Gallery (Nasjonalgalleriet):
Art lovers should also visit the National Gallery, which houses an impressive collection of Norwegian and international art, including works by celebrated artists such as Johan Christian Dahl and Harald Sohlberg.

10. Aker Brygge and Tjuvholmen:
Aker Brygge is a lively waterfront area with a mix of restaurants, shops, and entertainment venues. Adjacent to it, Tjuvholmen offers contemporary art galleries, upscale boutiques, and stylish waterfront dining options.

These must-visit attractions in Oslo offer a glimpse into Norway's history, art, and culture, making your visit to the capital city an enriching and unforgettable experience.

5.1.2 Family-Friendly Activities

Oslo, the vibrant capital of Norway, offers a plethora of family-friendly activities that cater to both children and adults alike. From interactive museums to outdoor adventures, the city presents a delightful mix of cultural experiences and outdoor fun, ensuring that families visiting Oslo have a memorable and enriching time together. Here are some top family-friendly activities to enjoy in Oslo:

1. Viking Ship Museum:
Step back in time and embark on a fascinating journey into Norway's Viking heritage at the Viking Ship Museum. Kids will be captivated by the well-preserved Viking longships and artifacts on display. The museum also offers interactive exhibits and storytelling sessions, making history come alive for young explorers.

2. Norwegian Museum of Science and Technology (Teknisk Museum):
The Teknisk Museum is a wonderland of hands-on exhibits, engaging demonstrations, and interactive activities. Kids can explore science and technology through play, with sections dedicated to robotics, aviation, energy, and more. The museum also features a planetarium and outdoor play areas, ensuring a full day of educational fun.

3. Oslo City Museum:
Immerse your family in Oslo's history and culture at the Oslo City Museum (Bymuseet). The museum houses a diverse collection of exhibits, including artifacts from daily life in the city throughout different eras. The "Oslo Time Machine" exhibit uses virtual reality to transport visitors back in time to experience Oslo's past in a captivating and interactive way.

4. Vigeland Sculpture Park:
Located within the larger Frogner Park, Vigeland Sculpture Park is a must-visit for families. The park is adorned with over 200 unique sculptures created by renowned artist Gustav Vigeland, showcasing the human form in various poses and emotions. Children will enjoy running and playing among the sculptures, making it a great spot for a family picnic.

5. Oslo Reptile Park (Reptilpark):
For young animal enthusiasts, the Oslo Reptile Park offers a chance to get up close and personal with a variety of reptiles and amphibians. From snakes and lizards to turtles and crocodiles, this unique attraction provides an educational and thrilling experience for visitors of all ages.

6. Oslo Winter Park (Vinterpark):
If you're visiting Oslo during the winter months, head to Oslo Winter Park for some family-friendly skiing and snowboarding. The park offers slopes suited for all skill levels, including beginners, and provides equipment rental and lessons for those new to winter sports.

7. Outdoor Adventures in Oslomarka:
Explore the great outdoors with your family in Oslomarka, the extensive forested area surrounding Oslo. There are numerous hiking trails suitable for families, as well as scenic lakes where you can enjoy a leisurely picnic or go fishing. During the warmer months, you can also rent bikes and explore the forest on two wheels.

8. The Norwegian National Opera & Ballet:
Introduce your children to the world of performing arts by attending a family-friendly opera or ballet performance at the Norwegian National Opera & Ballet. The stunning modern architecture of the opera house is an attraction in itself, and the performances offer a unique cultural experience for the whole family.

Oslo's family-friendly activities ensure that every member of the family can enjoy a fulfilling and engaging vacation. From learning about Norway's history to exploring the wonders of science, and from playing among sculptures to embracing outdoor adventures, Oslo offers an unforgettable journey of discovery for families traveling with kids.

5.1.3 Romantic Experiences for Couples

Oslo, Norway's vibrant and cosmopolitan capital, offers a delightful array of romantic experiences for couples seeking to kindle their love amidst the city's charming ambiance and scenic beauty. From leisurely strolls along picturesque waterfronts to candlelit dinners with breathtaking views, Oslo promises to create cherished memories that will last a lifetime.

1. Vigeland Park and the Love Bridge:
Begin your romantic escapade in Vigeland Park, the world's largest sculpture park created by a single artist, Gustav Vigeland. The park is adorned with over 200 bronze and granite sculptures, depicting the various stages of love and the human experience. Wander hand-in-hand among the intricate statues, and don't miss the iconic "Monolith" centerpiece. Before leaving the park,

visit the Love Bridge, a popular spot where couples place padlocks symbolizing their eternal love.

2. Oslo Fjord Cruise:
Embark on a magical cruise along the serene waters of the Oslo Fjord, taking in the stunning views of the city's coastline and surrounding islands. Several tour operators offer romantic evening cruises, complete with candlelit dinners and the opportunity to witness the sun setting over the horizon, casting a warm glow over the city's skyline.

3. Sunset at Ekebergparken Sculpture Park:
Ekebergparken Sculpture Park is not only a treasure trove of contemporary art but also an idyllic location to catch a mesmerizing sunset with your significant other. Find a secluded spot atop the park's hill, overlooking Oslo's harbor, and revel in the breathtaking hues of the twilight sky.

4. Opera and Ballet at the Oslo Opera House:
For a touch of elegance and cultural sophistication, attend a ballet or opera performance at the Oslo Opera House. The striking architecture of the building allows visitors to walk on its roof, providing panoramic views of the city. A romantic evening spent watching a world-class performance

against the backdrop of the sparkling city lights is an experience to cherish.

5. Cozy Cafés and Intimate Dining:
Oslo is dotted with charming cafés and restaurants that exude warmth and intimacy. Enjoy a leisurely breakfast at one of the city's inviting coffee houses, or opt for a cozy dinner by candlelight at a restaurant overlooking the fjord. For a unique experience, book a table at one of the floating restaurants, where you can savor delicious Norwegian cuisine while gently rocking on the water.

6. Akershus Fortress and Castle:
Step back in time with a visit to the historic Akershus Fortress and Castle. Explore the well-preserved medieval architecture, wander hand-in-hand through the fortress grounds, and admire the panoramic views of the city and the fjord. The tranquil atmosphere creates the perfect setting for an intimate stroll with your loved one.

7. Romantic Winter Adventures:
If you're visiting Oslo during the winter months, embrace the romantic charm of the snowy season. Take a horse-drawn carriage ride through the city's cobblestone streets, indulge in hot chocolate at cozy

cafes, or embrace the Norwegian tradition of koselig (coziness) by snuggling up together near a fireplace.

In Oslo, romance is found in every corner, whether it's within the embrace of its nature, the charm of its architecture, or the heartwarming hospitality of its people. Embrace the magic of this vibrant city and create unforgettable moments with your beloved as you explore its romantic offerings.

5.2 Bergen

Nestled between the majestic fjords and surrounded by seven mountains, Bergen stands as a captivating gateway to the natural wonders of Norway. As the country's second-largest city and a UNESCO World Heritage site, Bergen exudes a unique charm that has enchanted travelers for centuries. With its rich maritime history, colorful wooden houses, and vibrant cultural scene, this coastal gem offers a perfect blend of traditional heritage and contemporary delights.

Historical Charms:
Bergen's history dates back to the Viking Age, and the city's Hanseatic Wharf, known as Bryggen, is a testament to its past. The iconic row of colorful wooden buildings, dating back to the 14th century,

has been lovingly restored and now houses shops, galleries, and eateries. Strolling through Bryggen's narrow alleyways feels like stepping back in time, as the scent of tarred wood and the creaking of old floorboards evoke the city's maritime legacy.

Bryggen also hosts the Hanseatic Museum, where visitors can delve into the lives of the Hanseatic merchants who traded goods in the region during the Middle Ages. The museum provides a fascinating glimpse into Bergen's trading history and the challenges faced by the traders in this northern outpost.

Scenic Delights:
Surrounded by stunning natural beauty, Bergen offers a myriad of scenic experiences. Fløyen, one of the city's seven mountains, is a favorite among both locals and tourists. A funicular ride to the top rewards visitors with panoramic views of the city, fjords, and distant mountains. Hiking enthusiasts can also explore the hiking trails that crisscross the mountains, offering opportunities to connect with nature and enjoy breathtaking vistas.

Bergen's waterfront adds to the city's allure, with bustling harbors and maritime activities. Take a leisurely stroll along the waterfront, where fishing boats and sailboats bob on the waves, and enjoy a fresh seafood meal while gazing out at the fjords. Visitors can also hop on a boat tour to explore nearby fjords like Nærøyfjord and Sognefjord, both of which offer awe-inspiring vistas and a chance to witness Norway's dramatic landscapes up close.

Cultural Treasures:
Beyond its natural splendor, Bergen is a cultural hub that celebrates arts and music. The city hosts numerous festivals and events throughout the year, including the renowned Bergen International Festival, which attracts artists and performers from around the world. Art enthusiasts can visit the KODE Art Museums, a collection of four museums featuring works by famous Norwegian artists such as Edvard Munch.

Bergen's rich musical heritage is also evident through its vibrant music scene. The city has produced several influential musicians, including the world-renowned composer Edvard Grieg. Visitors can attend concerts at Grieghallen, a concert hall dedicated to his memory, or enjoy live music performances at various venues across the city.

A Gastronomic Paradise:

Bergen's culinary scene is a delight for foodies, with an abundance of fresh seafood and local specialties. The city's fish market, Torget, offers a vibrant atmosphere where visitors can sample an array of seafood dishes, including the iconic Norwegian salmon and traditional fish cakes. Additionally, Bergen's diverse restaurant scene caters to all tastes, from traditional Norwegian cuisine to international flavors.

With its history, natural beauty, cultural offerings, and delectable cuisine, Bergen beckons travelers seeking an authentic Norwegian experience. Whether you're exploring the charming Bryggen, embarking on fjord adventures, or immersing yourself in the city's vibrant arts and music scene, Bergen promises an enchanting journey that captures the essence of Norway's soul.

5.2.1 Notable Landmarks and Sights

Bergen, a UNESCO World Heritage City and Norway's second-largest city, is a captivating destination that delights visitors with its stunning landscapes, rich history, and vibrant cultural scene. Nestled between seven hills and surrounded by fjords, Bergen's unique geography provides the backdrop for a plethora of remarkable landmarks and sights. Here are some must-visit attractions that showcase the city's charm and allure:

1. Bryggen Hanseatic Wharf:
Arguably the most iconic sight in Bergen, Bryggen Hanseatic Wharf is a living testament to the city's medieval past. This historic district consists of colorful wooden buildings dating back to the 14th century, reflecting the architectural heritage of the Hanseatic League. Stroll through the narrow alleyways, now housing boutiques, galleries, and cafes, and soak in the ambiance of a bygone era.

2. Fløyen and Ulriken Mountains:
For panoramic views of Bergen and its surrounding fjords, take a funicular or hike to the summits of Fløyen and Ulriken. Fløyen offers an easily accessible vantage point, while more adventurous travelers can embark on a challenging hike to the top of Ulriken. Regardless of your choice, the breathtaking vistas of the city and the surrounding natural beauty make it a rewarding experience.

3. Fish Market (Fisketorget):
Located at the heart of Bergen's waterfront, the Fish Market is a bustling attraction that has been a vibrant trading hub for centuries. Sample a variety of fresh seafood delicacies, including salmon,

shrimp, and king crab, or browse through stalls selling local crafts and souvenirs. The lively atmosphere and maritime charm make this a must-visit spot.

4. Bergenhus Fortress:
A symbol of Bergen's historical significance, Bergenhus Fortress is one of Norway's oldest and best-preserved fortresses. Dating back to the 13th century, the fortress has played a crucial role in the city's defense over the centuries. Explore its medieval buildings, including the Haakon's Hall and the Rosenkrantz Tower, and learn about the city's tumultuous past.

5. Troldhaugen:
Music enthusiasts will be drawn to Troldhaugen, the former home of the renowned Norwegian composer Edvard Grieg. This idyllic residence, situated on the banks of Lake Nordås, offers an intimate glimpse into Grieg's life and works. Visit the composer's villa, the Grieg Museum, and attend concerts featuring his compositions in the stunning concert hall overlooking the lake.

6. Bergen Cathedral (Bergen Domkirke):
As one of the most significant churches in Norway, Bergen Cathedral stands as an architectural gem

and a religious landmark. Dating back to the 12th century, the cathedral features an exquisite Gothic design, intricate stained glass windows, and impressive stone carvings.

7. KODE Art Museums:
Art aficionados will be enthralled by the KODE art museums, a collection of four museums showcasing various forms of art, including paintings, sculptures, and crafts. The KODE museums hold an extensive collection of works by Norwegian artists like Edvard Munch and Nikolai Astrup, as well as international masters.

8. Gamlehaugen:
Experience a touch of royal grandeur at Gamlehaugen, the royal residence in Bergen. This stately mansion, surrounded by manicured gardens and a tranquil lake, serves as the summer residence for the Norwegian Royal Family. While the interior is not open to the public, the picturesque grounds are perfect for leisurely walks and picnics.

These notable landmarks and sights in Bergen weave together a tapestry of history, culture, and natural beauty. Whether you're wandering through the historic streets of Bryggen, immersing yourself in art at the KODE museums, or savoring the sights from atop the city's mountains, Bergen promises a captivating journey into Norway's vibrant soul.

5.2.2 Activities for Kids

Bergen, the charming coastal city on Norway's western shores, offers a treasure trove of engaging and family-friendly activities that will captivate the imaginations of children of all ages. With its vibrant culture, historical charm, and stunning natural surroundings, Bergen presents a perfect playground for young travelers. Here are some delightful activities for kids to enjoy while visiting this enchanting city:

1. Bryggen Hanseatic Wharf:
Embark on a fascinating journey back in time at Bryggen Hanseatic Wharf, a UNESCO World Heritage Site. Kids will be enthralled by the row of colorful wooden buildings, dating back to the 14th century. As they explore this historical area, they can learn about Bergen's seafaring past and the thriving trade that once took place here.

2. Bergen Aquarium:
A visit to the Bergen Aquarium promises a day of fun and discovery for the entire family. Home to a diverse range of marine life from the Norwegian coast and beyond, children can marvel at penguins,

seals, and sea lions. The touch pool allows kids to get up close and personal with creatures like starfish and crabs, providing a hands-on and educational experience.

3. Fløibanen Funicular:
For a thrilling adventure with breathtaking views, take the Fløibanen funicular to the top of Mount Fløyen. Kids will delight in the short but exciting ride to the summit, where they can enjoy panoramic vistas of Bergen and the surrounding fjords. The mountaintop playground offers plenty of space to run around, making it a great spot for a family picnic.

4. Bergen Science Centre - VilVite:
VilVite is a science center that sparks curiosity and creativity in children through interactive exhibits and engaging activities. Kids can learn about physics, biology, and technology through hands-on experiences, making it an ideal rainy-day destination for young learners.

5. Gamlehaugen:
Step into a fairytale setting at Gamlehaugen, the royal residence in Bergen. While the palace is not open to the public, the vast surrounding gardens are perfect for family strolls and picnics. Kids can

pretend they're in a royal castle while exploring the picturesque grounds.

6. Bergen Maritime Museum:
For little adventurers with a love for ships and maritime history, the Bergen Maritime Museum offers a fascinating collection of maritime artifacts and model ships. The museum provides insight into Norway's seafaring heritage and the importance of the ocean in shaping the nation's history.

7. Nordnes Park and Nordnes Sjøbad:
Nordnes Park is a lovely green space that provides a relaxing oasis for families. Kids can enjoy the playgrounds, run through open spaces, and even spot rabbits that roam freely in the park. If the weather allows, consider a visit to Nordnes Sjøbad, an outdoor seawater swimming pool adjacent to the park, offering refreshing splashes and fun in the water.

8. Bergen City Museum - Old Bergen:
Step back into the 18th and 19th centuries at Old Bergen, an open-air museum showcasing a reconstructed historical town. Children can dress up in period costumes and experience life in an authentic old-style Norwegian neighborhood.

Bergen's offerings for kids go beyond these activities, with plenty of local festivals, events, and family-friendly dining options to ensure a memorable and enjoyable stay for everyone. From its fascinating history to its embrace of nature and innovation, Bergen creates a magical experience that will linger in the hearts of young adventurers for years to come.

5.2.3 Romantic Spots for Couples

Bergen, with its stunning coastal setting and charming atmosphere, is a city that exudes romance at every turn. For couples seeking to create cherished memories in this picturesque Norwegian gem, there are plenty of enchanting spots that will captivate your hearts. Here are some of the most romantic spots and activities in Bergen:

1. Bryggen Hanseatic Wharf:
Start your romantic journey in Bergen at the iconic Bryggen Hanseatic Wharf. This UNESCO World Heritage site boasts a row of colorful wooden buildings that date back to the medieval times. Stroll hand in hand along the cobbled streets, exploring art galleries, boutique shops, and cozy cafés. The charming ambiance and historical significance of Bryggen provide an ideal backdrop for a leisurely afternoon together.

2. Fløibanen Funicular and Mount Fløyen:
Take a ride on the Fløibanen funicular to the top of Mount Fløyen, offering breathtaking panoramic views of Bergen and its surrounding fjords. The journey up the mountain is a romantic experience in itself, and once you reach the summit, you can enjoy a tranquil moment together while taking in the scenic beauty. Pack a picnic or savor a warm cup of cocoa at the Fløien Folkerestaurant, making this a memorable spot for couples seeking serenity amidst nature.

3. Lille Lungegårdsvannet Lake:
Lille Lungegårdsvannet is a picturesque lake located near Bergen's city center. Enjoy a leisurely stroll around its shores, hand in hand, as you marvel at the reflection of the surrounding buildings on the water. The area is beautifully illuminated at night, adding a touch of magic to your evening walk. It's an ideal spot for a romantic sunset or a quiet moment under the stars.

4. Fjord Cruise:
A visit to Bergen wouldn't be complete without exploring the nearby fjords. Embark on a romantic fjord cruise, where you and your partner can soak in the awe-inspiring scenery of steep cliffs,

cascading waterfalls, and tranquil waters. There are several cruise options available, including day trips to nearby fjords like Nærøyfjord, a UNESCO-listed fjord renowned for its beauty.

5. Gamlehaugen Royal Residence:
For a touch of fairytale romance, visit Gamlehaugen, the royal residence in Bergen. The beautiful mansion is surrounded by lush gardens and overlooks the sparkling Byfjorden. Enjoy a leisurely stroll through the well-maintained grounds or have a picnic by the water, basking in the regal ambiance and tranquility.

6. Evening Jazz at Torgallmenningen Square:
If you and your partner appreciate music and a lively atmosphere, head to Torgallmenningen Square in the heart of Bergen. During the summer months, the square often hosts outdoor jazz concerts, creating a perfect backdrop for an enchanting evening filled with music, laughter, and dancing under the open sky.

7. Sjøboden Brygge Wharf:
Located in the charming coastal village of Alvøen, just a short distance from Bergen, Sjøboden Brygge is a romantic waterfront area with a scenic pier. Enjoy a romantic dinner at the waterfront

restaurants while the gentle sound of lapping waves sets the mood. The beautiful combination of sea, boats, and charming wooden houses creates an idyllic setting for couples.

With its blend of natural beauty, historical charm, and warm ambiance, Bergen offers a plethora of romantic spots and experiences for couples to savor. Whether it's exploring historical sites hand in hand, embracing the tranquility of the fjords, or enjoying cultural activities together, Bergen promises an unforgettable romantic escape in Norway.

5.3 Tromsø

Welcome to Tromsø, a magical Arctic wonderland nestled in the northernmost reaches of Norway. Known as the "Gateway to the Arctic" and the "Paris of the North," Tromsø offers a unique blend of natural beauty, vibrant culture, and thrilling Arctic adventures that will leave you awe-inspired and enchanted.

Northern Lights Capital:
Tromsø is renowned as one of the best places on Earth to witness the mesmerizing Northern Lights, or Aurora Borealis. From late September to early April, when the nights are longest, the skies above

Tromsø come alive with dancing ribbons of green, pink, and violet lights. Witnessing this celestial phenomenon is an experience of a lifetime, and numerous tour operators offer guided trips to prime viewing spots outside the city.

Arctic Wilderness:
Surrounded by majestic mountains, fjords, and islands, Tromsø presents an unparalleled opportunity to immerse yourself in the raw beauty of the Arctic wilderness. Adventure seekers can embark on snowmobile safaris, husky sledding expeditions, or cross-country skiing excursions through the snow-blanketed landscapes.

Whale Watching:
Tromsø also serves as a premier destination for whale watching enthusiasts. From November to January, humpback and killer whales migrate to the waters around Tromsø, offering thrilling encounters with these magnificent marine creatures. Hop on a whale-watching boat tour and be captivated by the sight of these gentle giants gracefully gliding through the Arctic waters.

Midnight Sun:
During the summer months, Tromsø experiences the extraordinary phenomenon of the Midnight

Sun. From late May to mid-July, the sun never fully sets, casting a golden glow over the city and creating an otherworldly atmosphere. This unique natural occurrence allows for extended exploration and adventure throughout the day and night.

Charming Arctic City:
Beyond its Arctic wilderness, Tromsø boasts a charming city center filled with delightful surprises. Explore the vibrant streets lined with colorful houses, bustling cafés, and trendy restaurants serving delicious Norwegian cuisine. Visit the Arctic Cathedral, an architectural marvel with its iconic triangular shape and stunning glass mosaic, and take in panoramic views of the city and surrounding fjords from Fjellheisen, the cable car.

Cultural Richness:
Tromsø's cultural scene is as captivating as its natural wonders. The city is a hub for arts and music, with numerous festivals and events taking place throughout the year. Explore the Polaria museum, dedicated to the Arctic region's unique wildlife and culture, or visit the Polar Museum to learn about the daring Arctic expeditions that have shaped Norway's history.

Warm Hospitality:

Tromsø's warm and welcoming atmosphere is embraced by its friendly residents. The locals' genuine hospitality and their love for their Arctic home create an inviting environment for travelers to experience authentic Norwegian life.

The Arctic Adventure of a Lifetime:
Whether you're chasing the Northern Lights, exploring the Arctic wilderness, or immersing yourself in Tromsø's cultural treasures, this Arctic paradise promises an adventure of a lifetime. So, don your winter gear or bask in the Midnight Sun and let Tromsø work its magic on your soul as you discover the hidden gem of Norway's far north.

5.3.1 Northern Lights Viewing Points

Tromsø, nestled deep within the Arctic Circle, is one of the world's premier destinations for witnessing the mesmerizing Northern Lights, also known as the Aurora Borealis. This enchanting natural phenomenon paints the night skies with vibrant colors, casting a spellbinding spectacle that leaves travelers in awe. As you embark on your quest to witness this celestial dance, here are some of the best Northern Lights viewing points in Tromsø to maximize your chances of catching this ethereal display:

1. Tromsø Island:
Despite being a city, Tromsø offers surprisingly dark skies ideal for Northern Lights sightings. Tromsø Island itself provides several fantastic viewing spots within the city limits. The Telegrafbukta area on the southern coast is a popular choice, offering unobstructed views of the night sky over the open water.

2. Tromsø Bridge:
Crossing the Tromsøysundet strait, the Tromsø Bridge offers a unique vantage point to observe the dancing lights above the city. Stroll along the bridge's pedestrian path to enjoy an elevated view of the Aurora with the city lights serving as a striking backdrop.

3. Prestvannet Lake:
Located just a short walk from the city center, Prestvannet Lake is a serene spot for Northern Lights viewing. The surrounding hills offer a shield from artificial lights, creating a dark environment perfect for witnessing the celestial spectacle.

4. Sommarøy Island:
A scenic drive from Tromsø takes you to Sommarøy Island, known for its picturesque landscapes. The island's beaches and quiet coastal areas provide

splendid spots for a peaceful and uninterrupted Northern Lights experience.

5. Ersfjordbotn:
A short drive from Tromsø, Ersfjordbotn is a quaint village surrounded by majestic mountains and fjords. Head to the nearby beaches or find a spot along the shoreline to witness the Northern Lights shimmering above the dramatic landscape.

6. Kvaløya Island:
Venture to Kvaløya Island, "Whale Island," known for its rich natural beauty. The island's remote locations, away from the city lights, offer ideal conditions for an awe-inspiring Northern Lights encounter.

7. Aurora Basecamp:
Consider joining a guided Northern Lights tour at one of the dedicated Aurora Basecamps in and around Tromsø. These camps are strategically located in areas with favorable weather conditions, increasing the chances of a magical display.

Tips for Northern Lights Viewing in Tromsø:
- Check the weather forecast and Aurora activity predictions before heading out to increase your chances of a successful sighting.

- Dress warmly with multiple layers, as Arctic temperatures can be harsh during the winter months.
- Patience is key; the Northern Lights can be unpredictable, so allow ample time for their appearance.
- Avoid bright lights and refrain from using flash photography to preserve the natural ambiance and protect the dark skies.

Northern Lights viewing in Tromsø promises to be a truly unforgettable experience, immersing you in the wonder of nature's grand spectacle. So, bundle up, keep your eyes on the skies, and prepare to be captivated by the dancing lights of the Arctic.

5.3.2 Family-Friendly Arctic Adventures

Tromsø, the "Gateway to the Arctic," is a captivating destination that offers families an extraordinary blend of Arctic wonders and family-friendly adventures. Located in northern Norway, above the Arctic Circle, this vibrant city is surrounded by breathtaking landscapes and is renowned as one of the best places on Earth to witness the mesmerizing Northern Lights. Tromsø's unique combination of natural beauty and exciting activities makes it an ideal destination for families seeking a memorable Arctic getaway.

1. Northern Lights Safaris:
One of the most unforgettable experiences for families in Tromsø is the chance to witness the enchanting Northern Lights dancing across the night sky. Tour operators in the region offer family-friendly Northern Lights safaris where knowledgeable guides lead you to the best viewing spots away from light pollution. Children will be captivated by the mystical beauty of the aurora borealis, making it a magical family bonding experience.

2. Reindeer Sledding:
Introduce your little ones to a true Arctic tradition with a reindeer sledding adventure. A reindeer sleigh ride is a gentle and magical way to explore the snowy landscapes while learning about the indigenous Sami culture from the herders themselves. Children will love meeting these gentle creatures and hearing fascinating stories about the Sami way of life.

3. Dog Sledding:
Feel the rush of excitement as you embark on a thrilling dog sledding excursion through the snow-covered wilderness. Kids will be thrilled to meet the friendly and energetic huskies, who will

lead the way through the Arctic landscapes. Experienced guides ensure safety and fun for the whole family, making this a memorable Arctic adventure.

4. Arctic Wildlife Encounters:
Tromsø is a haven for wildlife enthusiasts, and children will be thrilled to spot Arctic animals like reindeer, elk, and seabirds. Join guided wildlife tours that take you to some of the region's best viewing spots, or visit the Polar Park Arctic Wildlife Center, where you can see wolves, lynxes, and bears in spacious enclosures.

5. Tromsø Arctic-Alpine Botanic Garden:
Take a break from Arctic adventures and let the kids explore the Tromsø Arctic-Alpine Botanic Garden. Despite its Arctic location, the garden boasts an impressive collection of plants, flowers, and herbs native to polar and alpine regions. It's an educational and enjoyable experience for the entire family.

6. Tromsø Science Center:
For curious minds and aspiring young scientists, the Tromsø Science Center is a must-visit. The interactive exhibits cover a wide range of topics, from astronomy and polar research to hands-on

experiments that spark curiosity and learning in both kids and adults.

7. Family-Friendly Accommodations:
Tromsø offers a range of family-friendly accommodations, including hotels, cabins, and guesthouses that cater to the needs of families with children. Many places provide amenities like family rooms, playgrounds, and on-site activities, ensuring a comfortable stay for everyone.

Tromsø's Arctic wonders and family-friendly activities make it an ideal destination for families seeking an unforgettable adventure. From witnessing the magical Northern Lights to meeting friendly reindeer and huskies, Tromsø offers an Arctic experience that will be treasured by the whole family for years to come. Whether you visit in winter to chase the aurora or in the summer to experience the Midnight Sun, Tromsø promises a memorable and magical family getaway in the heart of the Arctic.

5.3.3 Couples' Winter Escapes

Tromsø, the vibrant Arctic capital of Norway, is a dreamlike destination for couples seeking a winter escape like no other. Nestled amidst snow-capped mountains and surrounded by the vast Arctic

Ocean, this enchanting city offers a magical winter wonderland that sets the stage for unforgettable romantic experiences.

1. Northern Lights Romance:
Tromsø is renowned as one of the best places on Earth to witness the captivating dance of the Northern Lights. Imagine cozying up with your loved one under a starlit sky, waiting in anticipation for the shimmering green and pink hues of the Aurora Borealis to illuminate the night. Embark on a Northern Lights safari together, either by dog sledding, snowmobile, or guided tour, to discover the beauty of nature's celestial light show.

2. Chasing Arctic Sunrises and Sunsets:
In the heart of winter, Tromsø experiences polar nights, offering a unique opportunity to witness both Arctic sunrises and sunsets in the same day. Share a magical moment as you watch the sun paint the sky in hues of pink, purple, and orange against a backdrop of snow-clad mountains and frozen fjords. Capture these precious moments together, creating memories that will warm your hearts for a lifetime.

3. Husky Sledding Adventure:

Embrace the spirit of Arctic exploration by embarking on a husky sledding adventure with your partner. Mush through the serene winter landscape, guided only by the sound of the dogs' paws on the snow and the breathtaking scenery around you. This exhilarating experience will strengthen your bond as you work together to navigate through the Arctic wilderness.

4. Reindeer Encounters:
Connect with the Sami culture, indigenous to the Arctic region, and experience a reindeer sledding tour. Snuggle up in reindeer-skin blankets as you glide through the snow, pulled by gentle reindeer. The Sami guides will share their stories and traditions, providing a glimpse into the ancient way of life in the Arctic.

5. Cozy Cabin Retreats:
Escape the cold together by retreating to a cozy cabin tucked away in the snow-covered wilderness. Many accommodations in Tromsø offer intimate log cabins with warm fireplaces and private saunas, providing the perfect setting for relaxation and romantic moments. Snuggle up with a cup of hot cocoa or a glass of wine and watch the stars twinkle through your cabin's window.

6. Arctic Gourmet Dining:
Indulge in a romantic Arctic dining experience, savoring local delicacies that celebrate the region's unique flavors. Many restaurants in Tromsø offer exquisite seafood dishes, including freshly caught Arctic fish and succulent king crab. Enhance your evening with a candlelit dinner, gazing out at the icy landscape or city lights.

7. Arctic Spa Retreats:
Pamper yourselves with a visit to an Arctic spa, where you can unwind in heated outdoor pools and saunas while being surrounded by snowy landscapes. Let the tranquil atmosphere soothe your souls and create a blissful experience to cherish together.

Tromsø's enchanting winter landscape and the array of romantic experiences it offers make it a perfect destination for couples seeking an extraordinary escape. From witnessing the Northern Lights to embracing Arctic adventures, Tromsø promises to ignite the sparks of romance in the heart of the Arctic wilderness.

5.4 Trondheim

Nestled along the serene Trondheimsfjorden on Norway's central coast, Trondheim is a city that seamlessly marries its rich historical past with vibrant contemporary living. As one of Norway's oldest cities, Trondheim boasts a treasure trove of cultural landmarks, medieval architecture, and a welcoming atmosphere that beckons travelers from near and far.

Historical Gems and Landmarks:
At the heart of Trondheim stands the iconic Nidaros Cathedral, a majestic Gothic masterpiece and Norway's national sanctuary. Dating back to the 11th century, the cathedral is an enduring symbol of the nation's Christian heritage and serves as the coronation site for Norwegian monarchs. Visitors can marvel at the intricate stone carvings, medieval statues, and the awe-inspiring rose window, immersing themselves in centuries of history and religious significance.

Stepping back in time, a visit to the Archbishop's Palace Museum offers a glimpse into medieval life. The palace, once the residence of the Archbishop of Nidaros, now houses a captivating museum showcasing artifacts and archaeological finds that shed light on Norway's ecclesiastical past.

Colorful Wooden Architecture:

Strolling through Trondheim's charming streets, you'll encounter rows of colorful wooden houses dating back to the 17th and 18th centuries. The historic Bakklandet district, with its cobblestone streets and quaint cafés, exudes a cozy and nostalgic ambiance. Many of these charming houses have been converted into boutiques, art galleries, and lively restaurants, making it a delightful area to explore and indulge in local treats.

Cultural Delights and Modern Charms:
Beyond its historical allure, Trondheim is a vibrant cultural hub, bustling with music, arts, and academic life. The city is home to the Norwegian University of Science and Technology (NTNU), attracting students from around the world, infusing the city with youthful energy and innovation.

Art enthusiasts will find a haven at the Trondheim Kunstmuseum, where contemporary and historical art collections from renowned Norwegian artists are displayed. For music lovers, attending a concert at the Olavshallen, a modern concert hall with exceptional acoustics, is an unforgettable experience.

Relaxing Along the Riverfront:

The Nidelva River flows gracefully through Trondheim, providing a scenic backdrop to the city's activities. Taking a leisurely stroll along the riverbank or opting for a boat tour offers a fresh perspective of Trondheim's enchanting landscape. In summer, locals and visitors alike bask in the sunlight along the river, enjoying picnics and outdoor performances.

Delectable Culinary Scene:
Trondheim's food scene is a delightful fusion of traditional Norwegian flavors and contemporary culinary innovations. Restaurants and eateries offer a diverse array of dishes, from hearty seafood platters to inventive Nordic fusion cuisine. Don't miss the opportunity to taste local specialties like "klippfisk" (dried and salted cod) and traditional Norwegian pastries.

Festivals and Celebrations:
Throughout the year, Trondheim hosts a series of vibrant festivals and events that reflect the city's dynamic spirit. The St. Olav Festival, held in late July, commemorates the legacy of Norway's patron saint, St. Olav, with cultural performances, concerts, and religious processions.

Trondheim's charm lies in its ability to blend its ancient heritage with contemporary lifestyles, making it a city that captivates both history enthusiasts and modern travelers. Whether you're exploring its medieval landmarks, delving into its cultural scene, or simply savoring the relaxed ambiance by the river, Trondheim promises an enriching and unforgettable experience on your journey through Norway.

5.4.1 Historical Sites and Museums

Trondheim, a city steeped in history and culture, is a treasure trove of historical sites and museums that offer a captivating glimpse into Norway's past. As one of the country's oldest cities, Trondheim boasts a rich heritage, evident in its well-preserved architecture, ancient landmarks, and engaging museums. For history enthusiasts and curious travelers alike, exploring Trondheim's historical sites is an enriching and immersive experience.

Nidaros Cathedral:
The crown jewel of Trondheim's historical landmarks is the majestic Nidaros Cathedral, a masterpiece of Gothic architecture. This iconic cathedral, built over the burial site of St. Olav, Norway's patron saint and former king, holds significant religious and cultural importance.

Construction of the cathedral began in the 11th century, and over the centuries, it has been expanded and renovated, resulting in an awe-inspiring structure with intricate details and stunning stained glass windows. Visitors can explore the cathedral's interior, attend religious services, and learn about its significance in Norwegian history.

Archbishop's Palace Museum:
Adjacent to the Nidaros Cathedral, the Archbishop's Palace Museum provides insight into the city's medieval past and the role of the archbishops who once resided here. The museum showcases archaeological finds, artifacts, and exhibits that shed light on the daily life of the medieval clergy and the historical events that shaped Trondheim's development.

The Old Town Bridge and Burial Mounds:
Strolling along the picturesque Old Town Bridge, visitors are treated to splendid views of Nidaros Cathedral and the surrounding riverbanks. The bridge's proximity to the historical burial mounds adds an air of mystery and intrigue to the area. These ancient burial sites date back to the Viking Age, providing a tangible connection to

Trondheim's earliest inhabitants and their burial customs.

Ringve Museum:
Music and history converge at the Ringve Museum, which is a fascinating destination for music lovers and cultural enthusiasts. Housed in a beautifully preserved manor house, the museum showcases an extensive collection of musical instruments from various eras and cultures. Guests can enjoy live performances, interactive exhibits, and guided tours that highlight the evolution of music throughout Norway's history.

Sverresborg Trøndelag Folk Museum:
For an immersive journey into Norway's rural past, Sverresborg Trøndelag Folk Museum is a must-visit. Situated in a picturesque open-air setting, the museum features over 80 traditional buildings that have been relocated from different parts of the region to create an authentic historical village. Each building is meticulously furnished to depict various periods, offering a glimpse into the daily lives of Norwegians over the centuries. Visitors can participate in guided tours, workshops, and cultural events, making it an engaging experience for all ages.

Rockheim:

For a more contemporary twist on history, Rockheim is Norway's national museum of popular music. The museum showcases the country's musical evolution, from traditional folk songs to modern rock and pop. Interactive exhibits, multimedia installations, and iconic memorabilia celebrate the diverse musical heritage that has shaped Norway's cultural landscape.

Trondheim's historical sites and museums are a testament to the city's enduring legacy and provide a captivating exploration of Norway's past. Whether you're fascinated by medieval architecture, Viking history, or the evolution of music, Trondheim offers a journey through time that will leave a lasting impression on your travel experience.

5.4.2 Family-Friendly Entertainment

Trondheim, the historic and vibrant city located in central Norway, offers a delightful array of family-friendly entertainment that will captivate travelers of all ages. This charming city, known for its medieval architecture, scenic riverfront, and welcoming atmosphere, is a fantastic destination for families seeking to create lasting memories together.

1. Nidaros Cathedral and Archbishop's Palace:
Begin your family adventure in Trondheim by visiting the iconic Nidaros Cathedral, one of Norway's most impressive medieval structures. Kids will be awestruck by the towering spires and intricate architecture. The cathedral's interior holds fascinating historical tales, and guided tours are available to engage younger visitors with captivating stories from the past. Adjacent to the cathedral is the Archbishop's Palace Museum, where families can explore exhibitions on medieval life and the country's religious history.

2. Ringve Museum - Music and Musical Instruments:
For families with budding musicians or music enthusiasts, the Ringve Museum is a must-visit attraction. Located in a beautiful manor house, this unique museum houses an extensive collection of musical instruments from different eras and cultures. Interactive exhibits allow kids to try their hand at playing various instruments, making it an educational and enjoyable experience for the whole family. The museum's idyllic gardens and panoramic views of the Trondheim fjord add to the overall charm.

3. Trondheim Science Center (Vitensenteret):

Ignite your family's curiosity and passion for science at Trondheim Science Center. This interactive museum offers a hands-on approach to learning through numerous exhibits and experiments. Kids can experience the thrill of virtual reality, explore the laws of physics, and discover the wonders of the natural world. The Science Center is designed to engage and entertain visitors of all ages, making it a perfect spot for a fun and educational family outing.

4. Kristiansten Fortress:
For an outdoor adventure that combines history with stunning panoramic views, head to Kristiansten Fortress. This well-preserved fortress dates back to the 17th century and offers a unique perspective on Trondheim's past. Families can wander through the fortress grounds, climb its walls, and enjoy a picnic while soaking in breathtaking vistas of the city. The fortress also hosts events and activities for kids during the summer months, adding an extra layer of excitement to the visit.

5. Bakklandet and the Old Town Bridge (Gamle Bybro):
Take a leisurely stroll through the picturesque neighborhood of Bakklandet, famous for its

charming wooden houses, narrow streets, and cozy cafes. Kids will enjoy the delightful atmosphere, and parents can savor a cup of coffee while the little ones explore. Make sure to cross the iconic Old Town Bridge (Gamle Bybro), adorned with vibrant red paint, connecting Bakklandet to the main city center. The bridge provides fantastic photo opportunities and a chance to admire the serene Trondheim River below.

6. Marinen Park and Playgrounds:
When it's time for some outdoor play, head to Marinen Park, a beautiful waterfront park with open spaces for picnics and recreational activities. The park boasts multiple playgrounds, including climbing frames, swings, and slides, perfect for children to burn off some energy and make new friends. Marinen Park's scenic location along the river makes it an excellent spot for relaxation and family bonding amidst nature's tranquility.

7. Gråkallen Mountain and Tram Ride:
For families with older kids who love outdoor exploration, a tram ride to Gråkallen Mountain is a thrilling adventure. Hop on the historic Gråkallbanen tram line, which winds its way through lush forests and offers breathtaking views of the city and surrounding landscapes. Once at the

top, families can go for hikes, enjoy a picnic, and immerse themselves in the beauty of Trondheim's wilderness.

Trondheim's family-friendly entertainment options ensure that everyone, young and old, will have a fantastic time exploring the city's historical treasures, embracing its cultural richness, and creating unforgettable moments together. Whether it's discovering medieval wonders, engaging in educational activities, or simply enjoying the great outdoors, Trondheim promises an enchanting experience for families traveling with kids.

5.4.3 *Cozy Couple Activities*

Trondheim, the charming historical city located in central Norway, offers a delightful array of romantic activities that are sure to create cherished memories for couples seeking a cozy and intimate experience. From picturesque strolls along the riverbanks to exploring medieval architecture hand-in-hand, Trondheim has something special to offer every couple. Here are some enchanting activities to indulge in while visiting this romantic destination:

1. Nidaros Cathedral: Begin your romantic journey at the iconic Nidaros Cathedral, a masterpiece of

Gothic architecture. This stunning cathedral is not only a symbol of Trondheim's history but also a place of serenity and reflection. Light a candle together and bask in the tranquility as you explore the intricate details of this majestic structure.

2. Bakklandet: Wander through the picturesque streets of Bakklandet, an enchanting neighborhood lined with colorful wooden houses and charming cafés. Stroll hand-in-hand over the Old Town Bridge, offering delightful views of the Nidelva River, and enjoy a romantic meal at one of the cozy riverside restaurants.

3. Romantic Boat Cruise: Embark on a leisurely boat cruise along the Trondheim Fjord and experience the city's breathtaking scenery from the water. Snuggle up with your loved one and savor the serenity as you sail past lush landscapes and historic landmarks.

4. Kristiansten Fortress: For a romantic sunset experience, take a short hike up to Kristiansten Fortress, located on a hill overlooking the city. Witness the sun setting over the horizon, casting a warm glow on the cityscape below, providing the perfect backdrop for a heartfelt moment.

5. Bicycling in Ila Park: Rent a tandem bicycle and explore Ila Park, a lovely green space with winding paths and scenic spots. This leisurely ride through the park's tranquil ambiance offers a chance to connect with nature and each other.

6. Jazz Concerts: Immerse yourselves in the magic of live jazz music at one of Trondheim's cozy jazz clubs. The intimate settings and soulful melodies create an atmosphere of romance and relaxation, perfect for a date night.

7. Lerkendal Stadium: If you and your partner share a passion for sports, catch a football match at Lerkendal Stadium, the home of Rosenborg BK. Feel the thrill of the game together and share in the excitement of the crowd.

8. Tyholttårnet: Take an elevator ride up to the top of Tyholttårnet, the iconic tower that offers panoramic views of Trondheim. Share a moment of awe as you gaze upon the city's twinkling lights, making it an ideal spot for a romantic evening.

9. Spa Day: Indulge in a relaxing spa day at one of Trondheim's wellness centers. Unwind together with a soothing couple's massage or enjoy the

tranquility of saunas and hot tubs, ensuring a rejuvenating and intimate experience.

With its blend of history, scenic beauty, and welcoming ambiance, Trondheim provides the perfect setting for couples seeking a cozy and romantic getaway. Whether it's exploring historic landmarks hand-in-hand or savoring a sunset over the fjord, Trondheim will surely leave you and your loved one with cherished memories to cherish for a lifetime.

5.5 The Fjords

Among Norway's many natural wonders, the fjords stand as some of the most captivating and iconic landscapes in the world. Carved by ancient glaciers over millions of years, the Norwegian fjords present a breathtaking tapestry of steep cliffs, serene waters, cascading waterfalls, and verdant valleys. A journey through these majestic geological formations promises an awe-inspiring and immersive experience for travelers seeking to connect with the raw beauty of nature.

What are Fjords?
Fjords are long, narrow inlets of the sea that penetrate deep into the heart of Norway's coastal mountains. These striking features can extend for

tens to hundreds of kilometers, with towering cliffs rising vertically from the water's edge. The combination of saltwater from the ocean and freshwater from melting glaciers creates a unique ecosystem, fostering abundant marine life and creating an enchanting habitat for various species.

Top Fjords to Explore:
1. Sognefjord: Known as the "King of the Fjords," Sognefjord is Norway's longest and deepest fjord, stretching over 200 kilometers inland. The picturesque Nærøyfjord, a branch of Sognefjord, is a UNESCO World Heritage Site, surrounded by dramatic cliffs and lush forests.

2. Geirangerfjord: Another UNESCO World Heritage Site, Geirangerfjord, is renowned for its breathtaking beauty and is often considered one of the most spectacular fjords in the world. The Seven Sisters Waterfall and the Bridal Veil Waterfall cascade down the cliffs, adding to the allure of this natural wonder.

3. Hardangerfjord: Known as the "Queen of the Fjords," Hardangerfjord is the second-longest fjord in Norway, celebrated for its orchards, blossoming fruit trees, and picturesque villages. In spring, the region transforms into a colorful display of apple

and cherry blossoms, creating a magical atmosphere.

4. Nordfjord: Surrounded by glaciers, mountains, and fertile valleys, Nordfjord offers a rich blend of natural wonders and cultural heritage. The Briksdal Glacier, an arm of Jostedalsbreen, is a must-visit attraction, where visitors can witness the powerful force of glacial ice.

Exploring the Fjords:
A variety of ways exist to explore Norway's fjords, each offering a unique perspective on these awe-inspiring landscapes:

1. Fjord Cruises: A popular choice for travelers, fjord cruises take you deep into the heart of the fjords, offering breathtaking views of the steep cliffs, cascading waterfalls, and picturesque villages along the coast. Whether on large ships or smaller vessels, these cruises provide an immersive and comfortable way to witness the fjords' grandeur.

2. Hiking Trails: For those seeking a more intimate connection with nature, numerous hiking trails offer unparalleled views of the fjords from elevated vantage points. Trails such as the Preikestolen (Pulpit Rock) and Trolltunga present exhilarating

opportunities for hikers, rewarding them with stunning panoramas at the end of the journey.

3. Kayaking and Canoeing: Paddling through the tranquil waters of the fjords is an enchanting way to experience the serene beauty of these natural wonders up close. Guided kayak tours offer a peaceful and eco-friendly means of exploring hidden corners and secluded coves.

Best Time to Visit:
The fjords of Norway are accessible year-round, each season offering its own unique charm. Summer (June to August) is the most popular time to visit when the weather is mild, and the fjords are bustling with activity. However, late spring and early autumn also provide pleasant weather, fewer crowds, and the added bonus of colorful blooms or fall foliage.

Preserving Nature's Treasures:
As visitors, it is essential to appreciate and respect the delicate ecosystems of the fjords. Responsible tourism practices, such as following designated trails, not disturbing wildlife, and adhering to waste disposal guidelines, ensure the preservation of these natural treasures for generations to come.

Embark on a voyage of wonder and discovery as you immerse yourself in the breathtaking beauty of Norway's fjords. Witness the harmony of land and water, and feel the transformative power of nature in one of the world's most extraordinary destinations.

5.5.1 Exploring Norway's Fjords

Venture into a realm of unparalleled natural beauty as you embark on a journey to explore Norway's majestic fjords. Carved by ancient glaciers over millions of years, these deep, narrow inlets are among the most iconic and awe-inspiring landscapes in the world. Embarking on a fjord expedition is an essential experience for any traveler seeking to immerse themselves in the heart of Norway's pristine wilderness.

1. The Fjords: Nature's Masterpieces
Norway's fjords are a testament to the power and artistry of nature. Surrounded by towering cliffs and lush greenery, each fjord possesses its own distinct character, captivating visitors with its serene ambiance. Among the most famous are the Geirangerfjord, a UNESCO World Heritage Site renowned for its dramatic waterfalls and mirror-like waters, and the Nærøyfjord, the

narrowest fjord in Europe, flanked by soaring mountains.

2. Fjord Cruises: A Panoramic Perspective
Embarking on a fjord cruise is the quintessential way to savor the splendor of these natural wonders. Numerous tour operators offer boat excursions that navigate through the heart of the fjords, offering breathtaking views of cascading waterfalls, quaint villages nestled along the shores, and wildlife encounters. Relax on the deck as you bask in the serenity of the surroundings, and don't forget your camera to capture the postcard-perfect moments.

3. Active Adventures: Kayaking and Hiking
For the more adventurous souls, exploring the fjords through kayaking is an unforgettable experience. Paddle gently across the calm waters, allowing yourself to be enveloped by the tranquility of the fjord landscapes. Kayaking grants you the freedom to get up close to hidden coves, waterfalls, and secluded beaches inaccessible to larger vessels.

Hiking enthusiasts can also indulge in the beauty of the fjords by taking scenic trails that wind through the rugged terrain. Several well-marked hiking routes offer breathtaking viewpoints, rewarding trekkers with panoramas that seem straight out of a fantasy.

4. Experience Local Life: Visit Fjord Villages
As you traverse the fjords, make a point to visit the charming villages that dot their shores. These picturesque settlements offer a glimpse into the traditional Norwegian way of life. Interact with the friendly locals, indulge in local cuisine, and explore the quaint streets adorned with brightly colored houses. Don't miss the opportunity to try fresh seafood, a specialty of the coastal regions.

5. Off-the-Beaten-Path Fjords
While the Geirangerfjord and Nærøyfjord are some of the most famous, Norway is home to numerous lesser-known, equally stunning fjords that provide a more intimate and secluded experience. Consider exploring fjords like the Hjørundfjord or the Hardangerfjord for a quieter and more immersive encounter with nature.

6. Seasons of the Fjords
Each season offers a unique perspective on the fjords. Summer brings long daylight hours and lush greenery, ideal for outdoor activities and wildlife spotting. Autumn adorns the landscape with a vibrant tapestry of colors, while winter unveils a

serene wonderland with opportunities for skiing and, if you're lucky, glimpses of the Northern Lights.

Exploring Norway's fjords is an encounter with nature's grandeur and a voyage into the heart of the country's soul. Whether you choose a leisurely cruise or an active adventure, these ancient waterways will leave an indelible mark on your spirit and create memories that will last a lifetime. So, let the splendor of Norway's fjords envelop you as you delve into the realm of natural marvels.

5.5.2 *Family-Friendly Fjord Tours*

Exploring Norway's majestic fjords is a must-do experience for any traveler, and luckily, these scenic wonders are also accessible and enjoyable for families with children of all ages. Family-friendly fjord tours offer a fantastic opportunity to immerse the whole family in the breathtaking beauty of Norway's natural landscapes while creating cherished memories together.

1. Comfort and Safety:
Family-oriented fjord tours prioritize comfort and safety, ensuring that children and parents alike can relax and enjoy the journey. Most tour operators provide comfortable seating, sheltered areas, and

onboard facilities, including restrooms and snack bars. Additionally, life jackets are typically available for everyone, guaranteeing a worry-free experience on the water.

2. Engaging and Informative:
Family-friendly fjord tours are not just about cruising through stunning scenery; they are also educational and engaging. Knowledgeable guides often accompany these tours, providing fascinating insights into the geological formation of the fjords, local wildlife, and captivating folklore. Children will be captivated by the stories and facts shared, turning the tour into a learning adventure.

3. Wildlife Spotting:
Many fjord tours offer excellent opportunities for wildlife spotting. Keep an eye out for curious seals, playful dolphins, and an array of seabirds that call the fjords home. Some tours even venture into areas where whales are frequently spotted, giving families a chance to witness these majestic creatures in their natural habitat. Wildlife encounters like these create thrilling and memorable experiences for children.

4. Interactive Experiences:

Family-friendly fjord tours often include interactive experiences to keep young travelers engaged. Some tours allow children to steer the boat (under the guidance of the crew), while others may offer hands-on activities like fishing or crabbing. These interactive elements add a sense of excitement and adventure to the tour.

5. Photography Opportunities:
Norway's fjords provide a photographer's paradise, and family-friendly tours ensure that everyone has the chance to capture the beauty. Children can unleash their creativity and snap photos of the breathtaking landscapes, waterfalls, and charming villages they encounter during the journey.

6. Shorter Duration Options:
For families with younger children or those seeking a more relaxed outing, there are shorter duration fjord tours available. These tours still offer captivating views and memorable experiences while catering to the attention spans of the little ones.

7. Picnicking and Relaxing:
Many fjord tours make stops at picturesque locations, providing opportunities for picnicking and relaxation. Families can savor a packed lunch amid the stunning surroundings, fostering a sense

of togetherness and bonding amidst nature's wonders.

8. Child-Friendly Amenities:
Family-friendly fjord tours often take into account the needs of young travelers. Some boats are equipped with play areas or entertainment options, ensuring that kids remain entertained throughout the journey.

Whether you're exploring the renowned Nærøyfjord, Geirangerfjord, or any of Norway's other breathtaking fjords, family-friendly fjord tours offer an unforgettable adventure for all generations. As you embark on this journey together, you'll discover that Norway's natural wonders are not only meant to be admired but also to be experienced as a family, creating lasting memories that will be cherished for years to come.

5.5.3 Romantic Fjord Cruises

Embark on an enchanting journey of love and tranquility with romantic fjord cruises in Norway. These cruises offer couples an opportunity to immerse themselves in the breathtaking beauty of Norway's fjords while enjoying intimate moments in a setting straight out of a fairytale.

1. Captivating Scenery:
Norway's fjords are renowned for their ethereal beauty, with steep cliffs towering over crystal-clear waters. Gliding along the serene fjords, couples will be captivated by the dramatic landscapes, cascading waterfalls, and lush greenery that surround them. The tranquility of the fjords creates a serene ambiance, perfect for rekindling romance and making cherished memories together.

2. Intimate Settings:
Romantic fjord cruises typically feature smaller vessels or private charters, ensuring a more intimate experience for couples. This setting allows you to enjoy each other's company without the crowds, giving you the space to connect and savor the moment in seclusion.

3. Sunset and Midnight Sun Cruises:
The magic of Norway's fjords is magnified during the late hours of the day. Sunset cruises paint the skies with hues of orange and pink, creating a captivating backdrop for a romantic evening. Alternatively, during the summer months, couples can experience the surreal phenomenon of the Midnight Sun, where the sun never sets, casting a warm glow over the fjords, and providing an

unforgettable backdrop for a unique romantic cruise.

4. Gourmet Dining:
Many fjord cruises offer gourmet dining experiences onboard, presenting couples with a chance to savor delectable Norwegian cuisine while surrounded by stunning vistas. Enjoy a candlelit dinner under the stars, indulging in fresh seafood and local delicacies, accompanied by fine wines that enhance the romantic atmosphere.

5. Relaxation and Pampering:
Romantic fjord cruises often include opportunities for relaxation and pampering. Some cruises offer spa facilities onboard, where couples can unwind with massages and rejuvenating treatments as they sail through the picturesque fjords. Unwind together in the onboard Jacuzzi or simply lounge on deck while holding hands and taking in the beauty around you.

6. Wildlife Encounters:
Keep a lookout for wildlife during your fjord cruise. The waters around the fjords are teeming with marine life, and you may spot seals, porpoises, and even whales swimming gracefully alongside your vessel. These encounters with nature add an extra

layer of wonder and excitement to your romantic cruise.

7. Onshore Adventures:
Many romantic fjord cruises also incorporate stops at charming villages and picturesque towns along the fjords. Step ashore hand in hand and explore quaint Norwegian communities, taste local delicacies, and perhaps find a secluded spot for a romantic stroll.

Whether you're celebrating a honeymoon, an anniversary, or simply seeking to escape into a world of romance, a fjord cruise in Norway offers an idyllic setting for love to flourish. The combination of breathtaking scenery, intimate ambiance, and pampering experiences ensures that your romantic getaway on the fjords will be an unforgettable and cherished chapter in your love story.

Chapter 6. Family-Friendly Activities and Attractions

6.1 Wildlife Parks and Zoos

For animal lovers and families traveling with kids, Norway offers a fantastic array of wildlife parks and zoos that provide a chance to get up close and personal with native and exotic species in a natural setting. These parks not only offer educational experiences but also contribute to conservation efforts, promoting awareness and respect for the animal kingdom. Here are some must-visit wildlife parks and zoos in Norway:

1. Polar Park (Bardu):
Located in the Arctic region of Norway, Polar Park is the northernmost wildlife park in the world and a haven for Arctic animals. This expansive sanctuary is home to wolves, bears, lynx, wolverines, and reindeer, as well as the elusive Arctic fox. Visitors can embark on guided tours and wildlife safaris, where experienced guides offer insight into the animals' behaviors and adaptations to the harsh Arctic environment. Polar Park focuses on providing the animals with spacious enclosures that closely resemble their natural habitats.

2. Kristiansand Zoo and Amusement Park (Kristiansand):
A perfect destination for families, Kristiansand Zoo combines the excitement of an amusement park with the wonder of a zoo. Spread across 150 acres, the zoo houses over 100 different species from all corners of the world. Here, you can encounter lions, giraffes, zebras, and many other African animals in the savannah exhibit, while the Asian area features tigers, red pandas, and elephants. The zoo emphasizes conservation and participates in breeding programs for endangered species.

3. Langedrag Nature Park (Tunhovd):
Langedrag Nature Park is a unique wildlife and cultural experience set in the stunning scenery of the Norwegian mountains. The park focuses on preserving and promoting the country's native animal breeds, including the majestic Norwegian Fjord horse, the iconic Norwegian Forest cat, and various farm animals. Visitors can take part in guided tours, wildlife safaris, and educational programs, where they can learn about traditional Norwegian farm life and the importance of biodiversity conservation.

4. Orsa Rovdjurspark (Sweden-Norway border):

While technically located in Sweden, Orsa Rovdjurspark is easily accessible from Norway's Trondheim region. This wildlife park is famous for its impressive collection of large predators, such as brown bears, Siberian tigers, Arctic foxes, and wolves. The park emphasizes the importance of preserving these top predators in their natural habitats and offers an opportunity to see these magnificent creatures in carefully designed enclosures that mimic their wild environments.

5. Arctic Wildlife Centre (Lofoten Islands): Situated in the stunning Lofoten archipelago, the Arctic Wildlife Centre focuses on showcasing the region's diverse marine life. Here, visitors can learn about Arctic seabirds, seals, otters, and other marine creatures that inhabit Norway's northern waters. The center aims to educate visitors about the fragile Arctic ecosystem and the importance of responsible environmental practices.

Visiting these wildlife parks and zoos in Norway is not only a thrilling experience but also a chance to connect with nature and support important conservation efforts. Whether you're traveling with kids or simply seeking to immerse yourself in the wonders of the animal kingdom, these attractions offer a memorable and educational adventure.

6.2 Amusement Parks and Adventure Centers

For thrill-seekers and families seeking exhilarating experiences, Norway offers a variety of amusement parks and adventure centers that promise adrenaline-pumping fun and memorable moments. From heart-racing roller coasters to immersive nature-based activities, these attractions cater to visitors of all ages, making them an essential part of any Norway travel itinerary.

1. Tusenfryd:
Located just outside Oslo, Tusenfryd is Norway's largest amusement park and a paradise for adrenaline junkies. The park boasts a fantastic array of rides, including roller coasters like "SpeedMonster" and "ThunderCoaster," along with water rides, carousels, and gentle attractions for younger visitors. Tusenfryd's thrilling mix of entertainment and lush surroundings makes it a top choice for families and groups seeking a day of excitement near the capital.

2. Kongeparken:
Situated in Stavanger, Kongeparken is an award-winning amusement park that combines thrills with a touch of Norwegian history and folklore. The park's main attractions include "The

Mine," an interactive ride exploring the history of Norwegian mining, and "The Dragon Coaster," a family-friendly roller coaster. For an adrenaline surge, visitors can take on the "SkyCoaster," a giant swing that offers panoramic views of the surrounding landscape.

3. Hunderfossen Family Park:
Located in the picturesque Gudbrandsdalen Valley near Lillehammer, Hunderfossen Family Park is a fairytale-themed amusement park inspired by Norwegian folklore. The park's centerpiece is the majestic "Fairy Tale Castle," but the main draw for visitors of all ages is the "Trollfallet" log flume ride, offering a thrilling journey through troll-infested waters. Hunderfossen also features an ice hotel, making it a unique destination for year-round enjoyment.

4. Dyreparken:
Combining a zoo and amusement park experience, Dyreparken in Kristiansand is a popular attraction for families. The park is divided into themed areas, such as "Kardemomme By," based on a famous Norwegian children's book, and "Dyreparken Zoo," home to Nordic and exotic animals. Younger visitors will love "Kaptein Sabeltanns Verden," an immersive pirate-themed adventure land.

5. Voss Vind Indoor Skydiving:
For those seeking a different kind of thrill, Voss Vind in Voss offers an exhilarating indoor skydiving experience. This state-of-the-art wind tunnel creates a controlled vertical airflow, allowing visitors to experience the sensation of freefall without jumping from an airplane. Whether you're a seasoned skydiver or a first-timer, Voss Vind provides an unforgettable and safe adventure.

6. Høyt & Lavt Climbing Parks:
Adventure lovers can test their skills and bravery at various Høyt & Lavt Climbing Parks scattered across Norway. These treetop adventure parks offer a range of challenging courses, featuring ziplines, rope bridges, and suspended obstacles. Each park is set amidst beautiful forest landscapes, providing a thrilling, nature-based experience for the whole family.

As you embark on your Norway adventure, be sure to include a visit to these amusement parks and adventure centers. From classic roller coasters and fairy tale-themed attractions to indoor skydiving and treetop challenges, Norway's offerings promise endless excitement and unforgettable memories for travelers of all ages.

6.3 Interactive Museums and Science Centers

Norway is home to a fascinating array of interactive museums and science centers that engage visitors of all ages in immersive and educational experiences. These institutions combine entertainment with learning, making them perfect destinations for families, curious travelers, and science enthusiasts alike. From uncovering the secrets of the universe to exploring the depths of the ocean, these interactive venues offer a captivating journey through the realms of science, technology, and culture.

1. The Norwegian Museum of Science and Technology (Teknisk Museum) - Oslo:
Located in the capital city of Oslo, the Norwegian Museum of Science and Technology is a must-visit for science enthusiasts. This interactive museum showcases the country's technological advancements and scientific achievements throughout history. Explore hands-on exhibits that delve into various scientific disciplines, including physics, astronomy, biology, and engineering. Children and adults alike can participate in interactive workshops, experiments, and demonstrations, sparking a sense of wonder and curiosity.

2. The Norwegian Petroleum Museum - Stavanger:
Situated in Stavanger, a city known for its oil industry, the Norwegian Petroleum Museum offers an insightful and interactive journey into the world of offshore oil exploration. The museum's innovative exhibits allow visitors to experience the challenges and triumphs of the oil industry through simulators, interactive games, and engaging multimedia displays. Learn about the geology of oil, the engineering behind drilling, and the environmental impact of oil production, all while gaining a deeper understanding of Norway's significant role in the global energy sector.

3. VilVite Science Center - Bergen:
VilVite Science Center in Bergen is a haven for inquisitive minds, especially for families traveling with children. This state-of-the-art science center offers over 100 interactive exhibits that encourage visitors to experiment, solve puzzles, and unravel scientific mysteries. Engage in activities related to robotics, physics, chemistry, and space exploration. The center also hosts exciting shows and demonstrations, making learning both entertaining and informative.

4. The Norwegian Maritime Museum - Oslo:

Located on Bygdøy Peninsula in Oslo, the Norwegian Maritime Museum presents an engaging exploration of Norway's maritime history and culture. The museum's interactive displays allow visitors to steer a virtual ship, experience a simulated sea voyage, and understand the challenges faced by sailors throughout history. Discover the evolution of shipbuilding, maritime trade, and Arctic exploration through captivating exhibits and multimedia presentations.

5. The Lofoten Aquarium - Kabelvåg:
For those exploring the beautiful Lofoten Islands, the Lofoten Aquarium in Kabelvåg offers a unique opportunity to learn about the region's rich marine life and coastal ecosystems. The aquarium features interactive tanks and touch pools that allow visitors to get up close and personal with various sea creatures, including fish, crabs, and even seals. Learn about the delicate balance of marine ecosystems and the importance of conservation efforts to protect Norway's stunning coastal biodiversity.

6. The Norwegian Glacier Museum - Fjærland:
Nestled in the charming village of Fjærland, the Norwegian Glacier Museum is a captivating ode to glaciers and their impact on the natural world.

Interactive exhibits here provide insights into glaciology, climate change, and the history of glaciers in Norway. A highlight of the museum is its 4D theater experience, where visitors can virtually explore the icy wonders of Jostedalsbreen, mainland Europe's largest glacier.

These interactive museums and science centers in Norway offer engaging and educational experiences that ignite curiosity and inspire a deeper appreciation for science, technology, and cultural heritage. Whether you're traveling with kids or seeking to satisfy your own thirst for knowledge, these institutions promise an enriching and unforgettable journey into the realms of discovery.

6.4 Outdoor Recreation and Hiking for Families

Norway's majestic landscapes and pristine wilderness provide the perfect playground for families seeking unforgettable outdoor adventures. From the youngest explorers to seasoned hikers, Norway offers a wide array of family-friendly activities and hiking trails suitable for all ages and skill levels. Immerse yourselves in the wonders of nature and create cherished memories that will last a lifetime.

Family-Friendly Hiking Trails:
Norway boasts an extensive network of hiking trails that cater to families with kids. Many of these trails are well-marked and easily accessible, ensuring a safe and enjoyable experience for everyone. Whether you're looking for short, leisurely walks or more challenging hikes, you'll find options to suit your preferences.

One of the most popular family-friendly hikes is the Rallarvegen Trail, also known as the Navvies' Road. This gentle path takes you through breathtaking scenery and historic railway tracks, providing an excellent opportunity for kids to learn about Norway's railway history while enjoying the outdoors.

Another family favorite is the Fløyen hike in Bergen. Accessible by a funicular or on foot, this trail leads to the iconic Fløyen viewpoint, offering panoramic views of the city and surrounding fjords. Children will love spotting trolls along the way, a nod to Norway's rich folklore.

National Parks and Nature Reserves:
Norway is home to several national parks and nature reserves that cater to families seeking a deeper connection with nature. The Jotunheimen

National Park, known as the "Home of the Giants," is Norway's largest national park and offers a diverse range of family-friendly trails. Hike to the serene Gjende Lake or explore the Besseggen Ridge, where children can marvel at the contrasting colors of the water and surrounding landscapes.

The Hardangervidda National Park is another family-friendly gem, characterized by vast plateaus and cascading waterfalls. The easy hike to the Voringsfossen Waterfall is an exciting adventure for kids, and the park's abundant wildlife provides excellent opportunities for spotting reindeer and other animals.

Camping and Family Adventures:
Camping in Norway is an ideal way to immerse your family in the natural wonders of the country. Norway's "allemannsrett," or "everyman's right," allows you to pitch tents in most uncultivated areas, making it easy to find a scenic spot for your family's outdoor retreat.

Many campgrounds and cabins are family-oriented, offering amenities like playgrounds, barbecue areas, and swimming opportunities. Share stories around the campfire, gaze at the starry sky, and let your children's imaginations run wild in the embrace of nature.

Marine Adventures and Fjord Cruises:
Norway's fjords are a sight to behold, and exploring them by boat is a must-do family activity. Take a family-friendly fjord cruise to witness cascading waterfalls, lush greenery, and charming villages nestled along the water's edge. Children will be enthralled by the mystical landscapes that often inspired fairy tales and legends.

For a more interactive experience, try kayaking or canoeing on the tranquil fjord waters. Many locations offer guided tours suitable for beginners, ensuring a safe and enjoyable experience for the whole family.

Safety and Preparation:
While Norway's natural beauty is captivating, it's essential to be well-prepared and safety-conscious when venturing into the wilderness, especially with children. Check weather forecasts before heading out, dress appropriately for the conditions, and carry essential items such as water, snacks, a map, and a first aid kit.

Keep in mind that some hiking trails may have age or height restrictions, so it's a good idea to research trails that best suit your family's abilities and interests.

In conclusion, Norway's outdoor recreation and hiking opportunities for families are boundless. The country's dedication to preserving its natural heritage makes it an ideal destination for families seeking to connect with nature and embark on unforgettable adventures together. Whether you're exploring majestic national parks, cruising through stunning fjords, or setting up camp under the Midnight Sun, Norway promises a family holiday filled with wonder, discovery, and cherished moments in the great outdoors.

Chapter 7. Romantic Experiences for Couples

7.1 Secluded Getaways and Romantic Retreats

For couples seeking an intimate escape in the lap of nature, Norway offers a plethora of secluded getaways and romantic retreats that promise to create cherished memories and strengthen the bonds of love. From serene coastal hideaways to charming mountain lodges, these dreamlike destinations cater to couples looking for privacy, romance, and the chance to reconnect amidst Norway's breathtaking landscapes.

1. Lofoten Islands: The Lofoten archipelago, with its dramatic peaks, white sandy beaches, and quaint fishing villages, is a postcard-perfect setting for a romantic escape. Stay in charming rorbuer (fisherman's cabins) nestled along the shoreline, offering cozy accommodations with stunning views of the surrounding sea and mountains. Couples can explore the islands hand-in-hand, embark on whale-watching excursions, and even go kayaking under the Midnight Sun for an unforgettable experience.

2. The Arctic Wilderness: For couples seeking an adventurous romantic retreat, Norway's Arctic region is a magical destination. Consider spending time in Svalbard, known as the "Realm of the Polar Bear." Stay in remote wilderness lodges or unique ice hotels, where you can cuddle up under the Northern Lights and embark on thrilling snowmobile safaris.

3. Geirangerfjord: Often regarded as one of Norway's most beautiful fjords, Geirangerfjord offers an idyllic setting for couples to bask in each other's company. Book a private cabin or a luxurious boutique hotel overlooking the fjord's turquoise waters and cascading waterfalls. Explore the region by hiking up to viewpoints or taking a peaceful kayak trip on the tranquil fjord waters.

4. The Norwegian Countryside: Embrace the tranquility of the Norwegian countryside by escaping to charming farm stays or historic manors. The Valdres region, for example, is known for its rustic allure and offers opportunities for romantic walks in the countryside, horseback riding, and tasting local delicacies.

5. Oslo's Romantic Hideouts: Even in the bustling capital city of Oslo, couples can find romantic

hideouts. Stroll hand-in-hand through the elegant Vigeland Park, home to numerous sculptures celebrating love and human connections. Opt for boutique hotels or bed & breakfasts tucked away in quiet neighborhoods, offering a relaxing ambiance for a romantic city break.

6. Fjord Cruises: Set sail on a private fjord cruise, where you and your loved one can soak in the tranquility of the Norwegian fjords from the comfort of a luxurious boat. Watch the ever-changing landscapes glide by, enjoy gourmet meals on deck, and relish each other's company as you embark on this romantic journey.

7. Private Wilderness Cabins: For the ultimate secluded getaway, consider renting a private wilderness cabin in Norway's vast natural landscapes. Surrounded by forests, lakes, or mountains, these cabins provide a rustic and intimate retreat where you can disconnect from the world and immerse yourselves in the beauty of nature.

Whichever secluded getaway or romantic retreat you choose, Norway's breathtaking scenery and warm hospitality create the perfect backdrop for a couple's escape. Let Norway's enchanting atmosphere kindle the flames of love and create moments that will be cherished for a lifetime.

7.2 Romantic Cruises and Boat Tours

For couples seeking an enchanting and intimate experience amidst Norway's stunning landscapes, romantic cruises and boat tours offer an unparalleled way to create lasting memories. Drift away on serene waters, with majestic fjords, charming coastal towns, and breathtaking panoramas as your backdrop, as you embark on an unforgettable journey hand-in-hand.

1. Fjord Cruises:
Norway's fjords are renowned worldwide for their ethereal beauty, and a fjord cruise is a must-do romantic experience. The UNESCO-listed Nærøyfjord and Geirangerfjord are among the most spectacular, with their steep cliffs, cascading waterfalls, and mirror-like waters. Many cruises offer candlelit dinners onboard, allowing couples to savor local delicacies while surrounded by nature's wonders.

2. Midnight Sun and Northern Lights Cruises:
During the summer months, Norway experiences the magical Midnight Sun, where the sun never sets below the horizon. Opt for a romantic cruise in the

Arctic regions to witness this natural phenomenon, with the sun casting a golden glow over the picturesque landscapes.

In contrast, during the winter, the Northern Lights grace the Arctic skies with their mesmerizing dance of colors. Couples can embark on Northern Lights cruises that venture into the darkness of the polar night, creating a fairy-tale ambiance as the celestial lights shimmer above.

3. Sailing the Norwegian Coast:
The Norwegian coastline stretches for thousands of kilometers, offering a multitude of sailing experiences. Consider booking a sailing trip on a traditional wooden sailboat or a luxury yacht, venturing through the labyrinth of islands and skerries along the coast. Explore hidden coves, remote fishing villages, and pristine beaches, stopping for romantic picnics and private moments amid the tranquility of the sea.

4. Lofoten Islands Adventures:
The Lofoten Islands, with their dramatic peaks and picturesque fishing villages, exude a captivating charm. Choose a romantic boat tour that navigates through the archipelago's crystal-clear waters, passing by red-painted fishing cabins ("rorbuer")

on stilts. These tours often include opportunities for fishing, wildlife spotting, and exploring secluded beaches, perfect for intimate moments.

5. Whale Watching Cruises:
Norway's coastal waters are rich in marine life, making it an ideal destination for whale watching. Embark on a private or small-group whale-watching cruise, where you and your partner can witness majestic creatures like orcas, humpback whales, and sperm whales breach and dive gracefully in their natural habitat.

6. Oslo Fjord Sunset Cruises:
For couples staying in Oslo, a serene sunset cruise on the Oslo Fjord is a romantic highlight. Sail past iconic landmarks like the Oslo Opera House, Akershus Fortress, and picturesque islands while the sun dips below the horizon, painting the sky with a kaleidoscope of colors.

7. Coastal Steamboat Cruises:
Embrace a touch of nostalgia by boarding a historic coastal steamboat that harks back to Norway's maritime heritage. These charming vessels offer scenic cruises along the coast, providing an authentic and romantic journey into the country's maritime past.

As you plan your romantic cruise or boat tour, keep in mind that the best experiences often require advance booking, especially during peak seasons. Whether you choose a short sunset cruise or an extended journey exploring the fjords and coast, Norway's romantic boat tours promise to create unforgettable moments, forging cherished memories with your loved one against a backdrop of unrivaled natural beauty.

7.3 Candlelit Dinners with a View

Indulging in a candlelit dinner with a view is a quintessential romantic experience, and Norway offers an array of enchanting settings that promise to ignite sparks of love and create cherished memories for couples. From charming coastal towns overlooking the fjords to mountaintop retreats with panoramic vistas, these dining spots provide the perfect backdrop for an intimate evening with your loved one.

1. Bergen - Bryggen Wharf:
In the picturesque city of Bergen, the Bryggen Wharf is a UNESCO World Heritage site and a charming location for a romantic dinner. Choose from a selection of waterfront restaurants and cafés that offer delectable seafood and Norwegian

cuisine. As daylight fades, the flickering candlelight sets a magical atmosphere, while the reflections on the water enhance the romance of the moment.

2. Oslo - Aker Brygge:
Oslo, the vibrant capital of Norway, provides a range of dining options, but none compare to the romantic ambiance of Aker Brygge. Overlooking the Oslo Fjord, this trendy waterfront area boasts a variety of restaurants and eateries where you can enjoy exquisite culinary delights while gazing at the shimmering waters and sailboats passing by. The twinkling lights of the city add a touch of romance to the entire experience.

3. Geiranger - Fjord Cruise Dinner:
For a truly unforgettable candlelit dinner with a view, consider a fjord cruise in Geiranger. Sail through the awe-inspiring Geirangerfjord, surrounded by towering cliffs and cascading waterfalls, as you and your partner savor a sumptuous meal served on board. The tranquil ambiance of the fjord and the serenity of the landscape create an idyllic setting for an intimate evening.

4. Tromsø - Arctic Fine Dining:

In the far north, amidst the land of the Midnight Sun or under the dancing Northern Lights, Tromsø offers unique opportunities for a candlelit dinner in an Arctic setting. Some restaurants in the region provide private igloos or cozy log cabins where you can dine in warmth and comfort, all while admiring the mystical Arctic scenery outside.

5. Lofoten Islands - Rorbuer Restaurants:
The Lofoten Islands are a haven for natural beauty, and the rorbuer (traditional fishermen's cabins) offer an authentic and intimate dining experience. Many rorbuer accommodations have on-site restaurants where you can enjoy locally sourced seafood and traditional dishes, all while gazing out at the stunning landscapes of the islands.

6. Trondheim - Overlooking Nidelven River:
Trondheim's picturesque riverside is a charming spot for couples seeking a romantic candlelit dinner. Many restaurants and cafés line the Nidelven River, offering delightful views and serene surroundings. As you relish the delicious Nordic cuisine, the soft glow of candles creates an intimate atmosphere, perfect for a romantic night out.

As you embark on your candlelit dining experience in Norway, be sure to book in advance, especially during peak tourist seasons. The settings and views are equally magical during summer's Midnight Sun or winter's Northern Lights. Whichever time you choose to visit, a candlelit dinner with a view in Norway will undoubtedly leave you and your partner with memories of an enchanting and unforgettable evening.

7.4 Couples' Adventure Activities

For adventurous couples seeking an exhilarating escape and a chance to create unforgettable memories together, Norway offers a plethora of thrilling activities that will ignite the spark of excitement and passion. Whether you're adrenaline junkies or simply looking to bond over shared experiences in the stunning Norwegian wilderness, these couples' adventure activities will take your romance to new heights:

1. Fjord Kayaking:
Explore the mesmerizing Norwegian fjords hand-in-hand as you embark on a kayaking adventure. Paddle through calm waters surrounded by towering cliffs and cascading waterfalls, immersing yourselves in the breathtaking beauty of nature. Guided tours are available for all experience levels, making this an accessible and intimate activity to share with your loved one.

2. Dog Sledding in the Arctic:
Experience the thrill of mushing your own team of eager huskies across the Arctic wilderness. In regions like Tromsø and Svalbard, you can join a dog sledding expedition that takes you through snow-covered landscapes, under the magical Northern Lights in winter, or amidst the Midnight Sun during the summer months. The bond between you, your partner, and the loyal sled dogs creates an unforgettable sense of camaraderie.

3. Hiking to Trolltunga:
For couples seeking a challenging adventure and jaw-dropping vistas, the hike to Trolltunga, or "Troll's Tongue," is a must. This iconic rock formation juts out horizontally over the Ringedalsvatnet Lake, providing a dramatic photo opportunity. The hike requires stamina, but the sense of accomplishment and the breathtaking scenery along the way make it a rewarding experience to share.

4. Arctic Wildlife Safari:
Embark on a thrilling Arctic wildlife safari in places like Svalbard, where you can spot polar bears, reindeer, Arctic foxes, and a variety of bird species. A guided wildlife tour adds an element of

excitement as you and your partner venture into the realm of Arctic fauna, capturing candid moments and creating lasting memories.

5. Rock Climbing in Romsdalen:
Romsdalen, located in western Norway, is a rock climbing paradise with its dramatic cliffs and challenging routes. This adrenaline-pumping activity encourages trust, communication, and teamwork between couples, fostering a deeper bond as you conquer the rugged Norwegian terrain together.

6. Northern Lights Chase:
Norway's Arctic regions, particularly Tromsø and the Lofoten Islands, are prime locations for witnessing the mesmerizing dance of the Northern Lights. Set out on a guided Northern Lights chase, where you and your partner can cuddle up beneath the celestial spectacle and revel in the magic of the Arctic night skies.

7. White Water Rafting:
For couples with a thirst for adventure, white water rafting in Norwegian rivers offers a thrilling adrenaline rush. Tackle the rapids together, laugh, and enjoy the exhilaration of navigating the wild

waters while surrounded by Norway's awe-inspiring landscapes.

8. Paragliding over Fjords:
Soar like birds over the majestic Norwegian fjords in a tandem paragliding experience. As you glide through the air, you'll witness the grandeur of the fjords and the sparkling waters below, creating an extraordinary moment of shared awe and wonder.

These couples' adventure activities in Norway offer the perfect blend of excitement, intimacy, and natural beauty, making them ideal for those seeking to infuse their romantic getaway with unforgettable thrills and exploration. With each heart-pounding experience, you'll strengthen your connection and return home with a treasure trove of cherished memories to last a lifetime.

Chapter 8. Norwegian Cuisine and Dining

8.1 Traditional Norwegian Dishes to Try

When visiting Norway, one of the most delightful ways to immerse yourself in the country's culture is through its traditional cuisine. Norwegian dishes are deeply rooted in the country's natural resources, reflecting its maritime heritage, agricultural abundance, and appreciation for seasonal ingredients. Here are some traditional Norwegian dishes you must try during your visit:

1. Gravlaks:
Gravlaks is a quintessential Norwegian delicacy, consisting of thinly sliced, cured salmon. The salmon is traditionally cured with a mixture of salt, sugar, and dill, and left to marinate for a few days. The result is a tender and flavorful salmon dish that is often served with a sweet mustard sauce and crispy bread.

2. Kjøttkaker:
Kjøttkaker, also known as Norwegian meatballs, are a comforting and hearty dish made from a blend of minced meat, typically a combination of beef and pork. The meatballs are seasoned with nutmeg, ginger, and allspice, giving them a unique flavor.

They are usually served with a rich brown gravy, boiled potatoes, and lingonberry sauce.

3. Raspeballer:
Raspeballer, or potato dumplings, are a traditional Norwegian dish with regional variations. They are made from grated potatoes mixed with flour, salt, and sometimes smoked bacon. These dumplings are boiled and served with a range of accompaniments, such as butter, bacon, and lingonberry sauce.

4. Fårikål:
Fårikål is considered Norway's national dish and is a simple yet hearty meal made with lamb, cabbage, and whole black peppercorns. The ingredients are layered in a pot and slowly cooked together, allowing the flavors to meld and create a deliciously tender and flavorful stew.

5. Klippfisk:
Klippfisk is dried and salted cod that has been a staple of Norwegian cuisine for centuries. This traditional preparation method allowed cod to be preserved for long voyages. Today, klippfisk is rehydrated and prepared in various ways, such as in stews or pan-fried with potatoes and bacon.

6. Rømmegrøt:

Rømmegrøt is a creamy sour cream porridge that dates back to Viking times. It is made from sour cream, flour, and butter, creating a rich and indulgent dish. Rømmegrøt is often served with a sprinkle of cinnamon, sugar, and a drizzle of butter, making it a delightful dessert or comfort food.

7. Lutefisk:
Lutefisk is a polarizing dish in Norwegian cuisine, with some adoring its unique texture and flavor while others find it an acquired taste. This dish involves dried white fish, typically cod, soaked in a lye solution to rehydrate it. The fish is then cooked and served with boiled potatoes, peas, bacon, and a creamy white sauce.

8. Krumkake:
Krumkake are delicate, thin, and sweet waffle-like cookies that are often served during festive occasions, such as Christmas and weddings. The batter is cooked on a special iron to create a crisp and intricate pattern. Krumkake can be filled with whipped cream, jam, or occasionally, savory ingredients.

When exploring Norway, don't miss the chance to savor these traditional Norwegian dishes. Each bite offers a taste of Norway's history, culture, and connection to its remarkable natural surroundings, ensuring an unforgettable gastronomic journey during your travels.

8.2 Recommended Restaurants and Cafés

Norway's culinary scene is as diverse and captivating as its natural landscapes. From fresh seafood sourced straight from the fjords to innovative Nordic cuisine, the country offers a delightful array of dining experiences for every palate. Whether you're exploring the cities or venturing into the countryside, here are some recommended restaurants and cafés that promise to tantalize your taste buds during your Norway adventure:

1. Maaemo (Oslo):
As one of Norway's most celebrated restaurants, Maaemo has earned three Michelin stars for its exceptional Nordic-inspired cuisine. Led by Chef Esben Holmboe Bang, the restaurant focuses on using locally-sourced, organic ingredients, many of which are foraged from the Norwegian wilderness. Each meticulously crafted dish tells a story of the region, and the dining experience here is nothing short of extraordinary.

2. Fiskeriet Youngstorget (Oslo):

For seafood enthusiasts, Fiskeriet Youngstorget is a must-visit. This seafood market and restaurant in the heart of Oslo serves up the freshest catches from Norway's coastal waters. Indulge in dishes like fish soup, fish and chips, and an assortment of delectable seafood platters. The casual atmosphere and sustainable sourcing make it a popular spot for both locals and visitors.

3. Bryggen Tracteursted (Bergen):
Located in the historic Bryggen area of Bergen, this restaurant offers a taste of Norwegian history. Housed in a charming wooden building dating back to the 18th century, Bryggen Tracteursted serves traditional Norwegian dishes with a modern twist. Try classics like bacalao (salted cod stew) or reindeer fillet, and enjoy the cozy ambiance of this historic gem.

4. Renaa Matbaren (Stavanger):
Chef Sven Erik Renaa's Matbaren in Stavanger offers a delightful blend of Norwegian and international flavors. With a focus on seasonal and locally-sourced ingredients, the restaurant's menu evolves throughout the year. Dishes are beautifully presented, showcasing the chef's creativity and passion for culinary excellence.

5. Lysverket (Bergen):
Located in the KODE 4 art museum, Lysverket is a restaurant that harmoniously combines art and gastronomy. Chef Christopher Haatuft brings his culinary expertise to the table, serving dishes made with sustainable and organic ingredients. The menu is ever-changing, inspired by the art exhibits in the museum, and the chic, modern ambiance adds to the overall dining experience.

6. Mathallen Oslo (Oslo):
For a taste of various Norwegian delights under one roof, head to Mathallen Oslo. This food hall is a gastronomic paradise, offering a wide range of culinary options, from traditional Norwegian cuisine to international delights. Sample cured meats, artisanal cheeses, fresh seafood, and more, all in a lively and bustling atmosphere.

7. Rorbua Pub (Svolvær, Lofoten):
If you find yourself in the picturesque Lofoten Islands, make sure to visit Rorbua Pub in Svolvær. Housed in a charming fisherman's cabin, this pub offers a cozy and authentic setting to enjoy local dishes like fish soup and stockfish, accompanied by stunning views of the surrounding mountains and sea.

8. Bakeriet i Lom (Lom):
No trip to Norway is complete without trying some traditional Norwegian baked goods. Bakeriet i Lom, located in the charming village of Lom, is a renowned bakery offering mouthwatering pastries and bread made with locally-sourced organic ingredients. Treat yourself to freshly baked cinnamon buns, sourdough bread, and other delectable treats.

9. Bølgen & Moi Briskeby (Oslo):
Nestled in a beautiful villa in the heart of Oslo, Bølgen & Moi Briskeby serves up a fusion of Norwegian and Mediterranean flavors. The restaurant's elegant ambiance and extensive wine list complement the culinary creations, making it an excellent choice for a special dining experience.

From refined dining to charming cafés, Norway's culinary landscape is a feast for the senses. Embrace the opportunity to savor the tastes of this remarkable country as you embark on a gastronomic journey through its diverse and delicious offerings.

8.3 Vegetarian and Vegan Dining Options

Norway, renowned for its seafood and traditional meat dishes, might not be the first place that comes to mind when you think of vegetarian or vegan cuisine. However, the country has seen a remarkable growth in plant-based eating, with an increasing number of restaurants and eateries catering to the needs of vegetarian and vegan travelers. Embracing sustainable and ethical dining practices, Norway offers a delightful array of vegetarian and vegan options that showcase the country's commitment to culinary innovation and environmental consciousness.

In larger cities like Oslo, Bergen, and Trondheim, vegetarian and vegan dining scenes have flourished, providing a diverse range of delicious plant-based dishes. Here are some of the highlights and tips for the vegetarian and vegan traveler in Norway:

1. Plant-Based Restaurants:
Major cities boast a selection of dedicated vegetarian and vegan restaurants that showcase creative and flavorful dishes. These establishments not only cater to vegans and vegetarians but also appeal to food enthusiasts seeking new and exciting flavors. In Oslo, you can find trendy eateries that specialize in plant-based burgers, sushi, and Mediterranean cuisine. Bergen and Trondheim also offer a variety of restaurants serving up

mouthwatering vegan fare, ranging from hearty soups to delectable desserts.

2. Vegan-Friendly Cafés:
Throughout Norway, you'll discover charming cafés that accommodate vegetarian and vegan diets. They offer an assortment of plant-based pastries, sandwiches, and salads, perfect for a quick bite or a relaxing afternoon break. Many cafés take pride in using locally sourced and organic ingredients, adding a distinct Norwegian touch to their vegan offerings.

3. Traditional Cuisine with a Twist:
While traditional Norwegian dishes are often centered around fish and meat, several eateries have ingeniously adapted them to cater to plant-based preferences. For example, you might find vegan versions of classic dishes like "lapskaus" (a hearty stew) or "grøt" (porridge), made with plant-based ingredients while preserving the flavors and textures that make these dishes beloved by locals.

4. Veg-Friendly Ethnic Cuisine:
Norway's multicultural cities have also brought a wealth of international cuisine to the table, and many ethnic restaurants offer an array of vegetarian

and vegan options. From Indian and Thai curries to Middle Eastern falafel wraps, you can indulge in a diverse range of flavors that cater to a plant-based lifestyle.

5. Farmers' Markets:
Exploring local farmers' markets is an excellent way to sample fresh produce and discover artisanal vegan products. Here, you can find an assortment of seasonal fruits, vegetables, homemade vegan cheeses, and plant-based snacks that showcase the country's agricultural diversity.

6. Sustainable Dining Practices:
Norway's commitment to sustainability extends to its culinary scene. Many restaurants and eateries place a strong emphasis on using organic, locally sourced ingredients, reducing food waste, and minimizing their carbon footprint. This ethos aligns perfectly with vegetarian and vegan principles, making Norway an ideal destination for travelers seeking eco-friendly dining experiences.

As Norway continues to embrace a more plant-forward approach to dining, vegetarian and vegan travelers can explore a delightful tapestry of flavors that highlight the country's culinary ingenuity and commitment to a greener future.

Whether you're a dedicated vegan or simply looking to incorporate more plant-based meals into your journey, Norway's evolving dining landscape will undoubtedly satisfy your cravings while showcasing the country's sustainable and compassionate approach to food.

8.4 Kid-Friendly Restaurants and Menus

When traveling to Norway with kids, finding family-friendly restaurants with menus to suit young palates is essential for a smooth and enjoyable dining experience. Fortunately, Norway is a welcoming destination for families, and many eateries cater to children with special menus and thoughtful amenities. Here are some tips and recommendations for kid-friendly restaurants and menus in Norway:

1. Children's Menus: Many restaurants, especially those in tourist areas and family-oriented establishments, offer dedicated children's menus. These menus typically feature a selection of dishes tailored to kids' tastes, such as simple pasta dishes, burgers, chicken nuggets, or fish and chips. These meals are often served in smaller portions and may come with a side of vegetables or fruit.

2. Pizza and Pasta Places: Pizzerias and Italian restaurants are popular choices for families with kids, as they usually have a variety of pizzas and pasta dishes that appeal to younger diners. Some places may even allow kids to watch their pizzas being prepared, adding an interactive element to the dining experience.

3. Buffets: Many family-friendly restaurants and hotels offer buffet-style dining, which is an excellent option for kids who may be picky eaters. Buffets allow children to choose from a range of dishes, giving them the freedom to pick their favorites.

4. Casual Cafés and Bakeries: Norwegian cafés and bakeries often serve sandwiches, pastries, and cakes that kids will enjoy. Traditional Norwegian cinnamon buns ("kanelsnurrer") are a particular hit with young ones.

5. Seafood Options: Norway is known for its delicious seafood, and many restaurants have seafood dishes suitable for children, such as fish and chips or fish burgers. It's a great opportunity to introduce kids to the country's culinary specialties.

6. Family-Friendly Chains: In larger cities and popular tourist areas, you can find international fast-food chains that offer familiar kids' menus, making them a convenient option for families on the go.

7. Allergy-Friendly Options: Norway is generally accommodating when it comes to dietary restrictions and allergies. Many restaurants label allergens on their menus, and staff are often willing to make adjustments to dishes to accommodate special dietary needs.

8. Play Areas and Entertainment: Some restaurants in Norway go the extra mile to ensure kids have a memorable dining experience. Look out for places with play areas, coloring sheets, or interactive games to keep children entertained while waiting for their meals.

9. Ice Cream Shops: Treat your kids to Norway's delicious ice cream, which is widely available throughout the country. You'll find a variety of flavors and toppings to satisfy every sweet tooth.

10. Picnicking: When the weather is nice, consider having a picnic in one of Norway's many beautiful parks or by the fjords. Supermarkets and bakeries

offer a wide selection of fresh, ready-to-eat meals and snacks perfect for outdoor dining.

Remember that Norwegian culture is generally child-friendly, and most restaurants and eateries will warmly welcome families with kids. Don't hesitate to ask for recommendations from locals or the staff at your accommodation, as they can provide valuable insights into the best kid-friendly dining options in the area you're visiting. Bon appétit!

Chapter 9. Cultural Experiences and Festivals

9.1 Norwegian Traditions and Customs

Norway's rich cultural heritage is deeply rooted in its traditions and customs, which reflect the country's historical and geographical influences. As you journey through this enchanting Nordic nation, you'll discover a tapestry of customs that have been preserved and celebrated by its warm-hearted people. Embracing these traditions will not only enrich your travel experience but also provide a deeper understanding of the Norwegian way of life.

1. Jante Law:
The Jante Law, or Janteloven, is a societal code of humility and equality that has long been ingrained in Norwegian culture. It discourages boastfulness or excessive pride and emphasizes the idea of "we" over "I." This egalitarian principle fosters a sense of unity and encourages individuals to value the collective welfare of the community.

2. National Holidays:
Norwegians celebrate various national holidays with enthusiasm and pride. Constitution Day, known as "Syttende Mai" (May 17th), is one of the most cherished celebrations. On this day, the

streets come alive with colorful parades, traditional costumes, and the waving of the Norwegian flag. It is a time for communities to come together and commemorate the signing of Norway's constitution in 1814.

3. Midsummer and Winter Solstice:
Norwegians hold deep-rooted pagan traditions related to the solstices. During Midsummer (around June 21st), locals gather to celebrate the longest day of the year with bonfires, dancing, and feasting. Conversely, the Winter Solstice (around December 21st) marks the shortest day, where communities light candles and create a cozy ambiance to combat the darkness of the season.

4. Hygge and Koselig:
"Hygge" in Danish and "Koselig" in Norwegian are similar concepts that emphasize coziness, comfort, and a feeling of contentment. These ideas are integral to Norwegian life, especially during the long winter months. Gathering with loved ones, enjoying hot beverages by the fireplace, and creating a warm atmosphere are essential aspects of this cherished tradition.

5. Family Bonding and Outdoor Activities:

Norwegian families place great importance on spending quality time together, often engaging in outdoor activities such as hiking, skiing, and camping. This appreciation for nature's beauty and the exploration of the great outdoors is ingrained in the Norwegian lifestyle, making it a family-friendly destination.

6. Coffee Culture:
Norwegians have a strong coffee culture, and coffee breaks, known as "kaffekos," are a cherished tradition. It is common for friends and family to gather over a cup of coffee and delicious pastries, fostering social connections and a sense of community.

7. Respect for Nature:
Norway's stunning landscapes have instilled a profound respect for nature among its people. You will often find an emphasis on sustainable practices and a commitment to preserving the environment for future generations. When exploring Norway's wilderness, following the principle of "Leave No Trace" is essential to maintain the pristine beauty of the countryside.

8. Sami Culture:

In the northern regions of Norway, you may encounter the indigenous Sami people, who have their unique customs and traditions. Sami culture revolves around reindeer herding, traditional clothing, and the mesmerizing art of joiking (a form of vocal chanting). Learning about and respecting Sami traditions is essential to promoting cultural diversity in Norway.

By immersing yourself in Norwegian traditions and customs, you will not only gain a deeper appreciation for the country's cultural heritage but also connect with the warm and welcoming spirit of its people. Embrace these customs, share in the festivities, and let the traditions of Norway enhance your travel experience in this land of natural wonders and enduring cultural pride.

9.2 Folk Festivals and Celebrations

Norway's rich cultural heritage is beautifully showcased through its vibrant folk festivals and celebrations. These lively and colorful events offer visitors a unique opportunity to immerse themselves in the traditions, music, dance, and cuisine that have been passed down through generations. Attending a folk festival in Norway is like stepping into a time capsule, experiencing the country's history and community spirit firsthand.

1. Constitution Day (17th of May):
One of the most significant and widely celebrated events in Norway is Constitution Day, known as "Syttende Mai." Commemorating the signing of Norway's constitution in 1814, this national holiday is a jubilant affair, observed with parades, concerts, and cultural displays in every town and city across the country. Children dress in traditional folk costumes, known as "bunads," while marching bands fill the air with lively tunes. The streets are adorned with Norwegian flags and buntings, creating a festive and patriotic atmosphere.

2. St. Hans (Midsummer):
St. Hans, celebrated on June 23rd, is a midsummer festival that heralds the arrival of the bright summer season. Traditionally, bonfires are lit on the shores of fjords and lakes, and people gather around to enjoy the warmth and light. It is a time for community gatherings, music, dance, and storytelling, creating a magical ambiance as the sun barely sets in the northern regions.

3. Olsok (St. Olav's Day):
Olsok, or St. Olav's Day, takes place on July 29th, and it honors Norway's patron saint, King Olav II Haraldsson. The Nidaros Cathedral in Trondheim,

one of the most important religious sites in Norway, holds a grand celebration with processions, religious services, and cultural performances. Pilgrims from around the world flock to Trondheim during this time, making it an excellent opportunity to experience the country's spiritual and historical traditions.

4. Riddu Riddu Festival:
Celebrating Sámi culture and indigenous heritage, the Riddu Riddu Festival is held annually in the village of Manndalen in northern Norway. This multicultural event showcases the music, art, and stories of the Sámi people, along with performances from various indigenous communities worldwide. Visitors can enjoy traditional joik singing, workshops, and exhibitions, fostering a deeper understanding of the Sámi way of life and its significance in Norway's cultural fabric.

5. Christmas Markets:
During the festive season, Norwegian towns and cities come alive with enchanting Christmas markets. Wooden stalls are adorned with twinkling lights, offering traditional handicrafts, local delicacies, and warm drinks like gløgg (mulled wine) and lussekatter (saffron buns). The aroma of cinnamon and spices fills the air, creating a

heartwarming ambiance to celebrate the holiday spirit.

Attending these folk festivals and celebrations allows travelers to witness the deep-rooted sense of community and pride that Norway holds for its traditions. It offers an opportunity to connect with locals, savor authentic flavors, and partake in centuries-old customs that continue to shape Norway's cultural identity. For visitors seeking an immersive and unforgettable experience, these festivals are an essential part of the Norwegian journey.

9.3 Art and Music Events

For art and music enthusiasts, Norway offers a vibrant and diverse cultural scene that seamlessly blends contemporary creativity with traditional expressions. Throughout the year, the country hosts a plethora of art exhibitions, music festivals, and cultural events that cater to all tastes and interests. Whether you're a fan of classical symphonies, experimental jazz, contemporary art, or traditional folk performances, Norway's art and music events promise to captivate and inspire.

Music Festivals:

Norway boasts a wide range of music festivals that cater to various genres and styles, attracting both local and international artists and audiences. Some of the most notable music festivals in Norway include:

1. Øya Festival (Oslo): Held annually in Oslo's Tøyen Park, Øya Festival is one of Norway's premier music events. It showcases a diverse lineup of local and international acts across genres like indie, rock, electronic, and hip-hop.

2. Bergen International Festival (Bergen): Known as "Festspillene i Bergen," this iconic festival is one of Europe's oldest, dating back to 1953. It celebrates classical music, opera, theater, dance, and visual arts, hosting performances in various historic venues throughout Bergen.

3. Pstereo Festival (Trondheim): Held in Trondheim, Pstereo Festival brings together a mix of renowned and emerging artists in the indie and alternative music scene. The festival's picturesque setting in Marinen Park enhances the experience.

4. Northern Lights Festival (Tromsø): Taking place in the Arctic city of Tromsø, the Northern Lights Festival celebrates classical and contemporary

music within the ethereal backdrop of the Northern Lights.

5. Nattjazz (Bergen): This annual jazz festival in Bergen attracts jazz enthusiasts from across the world with its diverse lineup of jazz, experimental, and avant-garde performances.

Art Exhibitions and Galleries:
Norway's thriving art scene extends beyond music festivals, with numerous art exhibitions and galleries that showcase local and international talent. Some notable art venues to explore include:

1. The Munch Museum (Oslo): Dedicated to the life and works of iconic Norwegian artist Edvard Munch, this museum houses the largest collection of Munch's paintings, drawings, and prints.

2. The Vigeland Park (Oslo): A unique outdoor sculpture park featuring the works of Gustav Vigeland, displaying over 200 sculptures in bronze, granite, and wrought iron.

3. The Astrup Fearnley Museum (Oslo): This contemporary art museum showcases works by prominent artists from the 1960s to the present

day, with a focus on contemporary Norwegian and international art.

4. KODE Art Museums (Bergen): Comprising four art museums, KODE offers an extensive collection of Norwegian and international art, including works by Edvard Munch and Nikolai Astrup.

5. The Nordnorsk Kunstmuseum (Tromsø): Located in Tromsø, this museum specializes in art from Northern Norway, providing insights into the unique artistic expressions of the Arctic region.

Street Art and Graffiti:
Norway's cities are home to impressive street art and graffiti scenes, reflecting the country's progressive and creative spirit. In cities like Oslo, Bergen, and Trondheim, you can find captivating murals and urban art that add a vibrant and dynamic element to the urban landscape.

Whether you're strolling through a contemporary art gallery or dancing to the beat of live music at a festival, Norway's art and music events promise to immerse you in the country's cultural richness. From the avant-garde to the traditional, the Norwegian cultural scene offers a delightful tapestry of experiences for art and music aficionados alike. Be sure to check local event listings and calendars to plan your visit and make the most of Norway's thriving cultural offerings.

9.4 Cultural Activities Suitable for Families

Norway's rich cultural heritage offers a plethora of engaging and educational activities that are perfect for families traveling with children. From interactive museums and historical sites to traditional celebrations, these cultural experiences will provide a deeper understanding of Norway's history, art, and traditions. Here are some delightful cultural activities that families can enjoy together during their visit to Norway:

1. Norsk Folkemuseum, Oslo:
Located in Oslo, the Norsk Folkemuseum (Norwegian Museum of Cultural History) is an open-air museum that offers a fascinating journey through Norway's past. Families can explore more than 150 traditional buildings from different regions, showcasing various architectural styles and domestic life throughout history. Costumed interpreters bring history to life, demonstrating traditional crafts, dances, and activities, making it an immersive experience for children and adults alike.

2. Vikingskipshuset (Viking Ship Museum), Oslo:
For families fascinated by Vikings, the Viking Ship Museum in Oslo is a must-visit. Kids will be enthralled by the remarkably well-preserved Viking longships on display, learning about the seafaring prowess and daily life of these legendary Norse warriors. Interactive exhibits and multimedia displays further enhance the learning experience, allowing young minds to step back in time.

3. Barnas Lekeland (Children's Playland), Bergen:
Barnas Lekeland is a cultural activity center in Bergen that caters specifically to families with children. The center offers engaging activities, workshops, and creative play areas where kids can learn about Norwegian culture through games, music, storytelling, and art projects. It's an excellent place for children to socialize with local kids while immersing themselves in Norwegian customs.

4. Christmas Markets:
If you're visiting Norway during the holiday season, make sure to explore the traditional Christmas markets held in various cities and towns. The markets are brimming with festive cheer, featuring handicrafts, local delicacies, and holiday

decorations. Children can enjoy meeting Santa Claus, sampling Norwegian sweets, and partaking in seasonal activities that showcase Norway's Christmas traditions.

5. Stave Churches:
Norway is home to some of the most impressive stave churches in the world, exemplifying the country's unique medieval wooden architecture. These historical gems offer an exciting opportunity for families to step into the past and explore centuries-old places of worship. Among the notable stave churches are the Borgund Stave Church in Lærdal and the Urnes Stave Church in Sogn og Fjordane, both UNESCO World Heritage Sites.

6. Local Festivals and Celebrations:
Throughout the year, Norway hosts a range of festivals celebrating its diverse cultural heritage. Families can join in on these festivities, such as the Midsummer celebrations (Sankthans), Sami National Day (Sámi álbmotbeaivi), and Constitution Day (Syttende Mai). These events feature parades, music, dance, and traditional costumes, giving families a glimpse into Norway's vibrant cultural tapestry.

7. Visit Sami Cultural Centers:

In Northern Norway, families can learn about the indigenous Sami culture, which has deep historical roots in the region. Sami cultural centers like the RiddoDuottarMuseat in Karasjok and the Sami Siida Museum in Kautokeino provide insights into Sami history, traditions, and contemporary life. Families can engage with Sami guides, try traditional foods, and even experience reindeer sledding.

Engaging in these cultural activities together as a family will not only create cherished memories but also foster a deeper appreciation for Norway's heritage and its place in the modern world. From Viking history to traditional celebrations, Norway's cultural experiences will captivate the young and the young at heart, making your family trip an enriching and rewarding journey.

Chapter 10. Outdoor Adventures and Nature Exploration

10.1 Hiking and Trekking Routes

For nature lovers and outdoor enthusiasts, Norway is a true paradise offering an extensive network of hiking and trekking routes that showcase the country's unrivaled natural beauty. Whether you're an experienced mountaineer or a casual hiker, Norway's diverse landscapes cater to all levels of adventurers, providing an opportunity to immerse yourself in breathtaking wilderness and stunning vistas.

1. The Norwegian Trekking Association (DNT) Trails:
The Norwegian Trekking Association, known as Den Norske Turistforening (DNT), maintains a vast system of hiking trails throughout Norway. These well-marked paths, often passing through idyllic valleys, lush forests, and pristine mountain plateaus, make it easy for hikers to explore the country's remote and scenic areas. The DNT cabins, strategically placed along the routes, provide shelter and comfort to trekkers, making multi-day hikes a popular choice for those seeking an immersive outdoor experience.

2. Besseggen Ridge, Jotunheimen National Park:
Located in the Jotunheimen National Park, the Besseggen Ridge hike is one of Norway's most famous and spectacular routes. The trail takes you along a narrow ridge with sweeping views of the Gjende Lake on one side and the Bessvatnet Lake on the other. The vibrant hues of the lakes against the dramatic backdrop of the surrounding peaks create an unforgettable visual feast.

3. Preikestolen (Pulpit Rock) Hike:
One of Norway's most iconic hikes, the Preikestolen hike near Stavanger offers an awe-inspiring reward at the end. The trail takes you to the edge of the famous Pulpit Rock, a flat-topped cliff towering 604 meters above Lysefjord. The panoramic views from the top are simply breathtaking, making it a must-do hike for visitors seeking an unforgettable vantage point.

4. Trolltunga (Troll's Tongue) Hike:
Challenging but rewarding, the Trolltunga hike is a bucket-list adventure for many. The trail leads to the iconic Trolltunga rock formation, jutting out 700 meters above Lake Ringedalsvatnet in Hardangerfjord. The stunning views of the fjord and surrounding mountains make the demanding ascent well worth the effort.

5. Romsdalseggen Ridge, Åndalsnes:
For experienced hikers seeking a thrilling adventure, the Romsdalseggen Ridge hike in Åndalsnes is a perfect choice. This challenging route offers dramatic views of the Romsdalen Valley, Trollveggen (Troll Wall), and the surrounding peaks. The trail's narrow and exposed sections add an extra element of excitement for adrenaline seekers.

6. Kjeragbolten Hike:
Located in the Lysefjord region, the Kjeragbolten hike is famous for the daring photo opportunity on a massive boulder wedged between two cliffs. The hike offers breathtaking views of Lysefjord and the Kjerag Mountain's iconic Kjeragbolten rock. The trek involves some steep ascents and descents, but the reward is a truly unforgettable experience.

Safety Tips:
- Before embarking on any hike, check the weather forecast and trail conditions.
- Bring proper hiking gear, including sturdy boots, waterproof clothing, and a map or GPS device.
- Always inform someone of your hiking plans and expected return time.

- Stay on marked trails and follow DNT's trail markings to avoid getting lost.
- Respect nature and wildlife, and adhere to Leave No Trace principles.

Hiking and trekking in Norway provide a soul-stirring connection with nature, offering a glimpse into the untamed wilderness that defines this captivating country. Whether you're conquering towering peaks or leisurely strolling through tranquil valleys, Norway's hiking routes promise unforgettable adventures and memories to last a lifetime.

10.2 Skiing and Snowboarding in Norway

Norway's winter wonderland is a paradise for skiing and snowboarding enthusiasts, offering a vast playground of snow-covered slopes, breathtaking mountain vistas, and a variety of thrilling winter sports. With its long snowy season and world-class resorts, Norway is a sought-after destination for those seeking an unforgettable alpine adventure.

Key Skiing and Snowboarding Regions:

1. Hemsedal: Known as the "Scandinavian Alps," Hemsedal is one of Norway's most popular skiing destinations. With over 50 slopes catering to all

skill levels, from beginners to advanced riders, Hemsedal offers a diverse array of terrain to explore. The resort town also boasts excellent off-piste skiing opportunities and a lively après-ski scene.

2. Trysil: Located in southeastern Norway, Trysil is the country's largest ski resort and a favorite among families and beginners. With well-groomed slopes and an array of ski schools and children's areas, Trysil ensures an enjoyable experience for all ages. More experienced skiers and snowboarders can tackle the challenging runs in Trysil's mountainous terrain.

3. Geilo: Geilo is a charming mountain village situated between Oslo and Bergen, making it easily accessible for travelers. The resort's gentle slopes make it an excellent destination for families and beginners, while the nearby off-piste areas and terrain parks cater to more advanced riders. Geilo also offers a range of off-slope activities, such as dog sledding and ice fishing.

4. Lillehammer: Famous for hosting the 1994 Winter Olympics, Lillehammer continues to be a winter sports hub. The region's ski resorts, such as Hafjell and Kvitfjell, offer an array of

well-maintained slopes and stunning views. Lillehammer is an ideal destination for families, as it offers a mix of family-friendly slopes and fun winter activities like tobogganing.

The Northern Lights Skiing Experience:

For a truly magical skiing or snowboarding adventure, head north to Tromsø and the surrounding areas. During the winter months, these regions are bathed in the ethereal glow of the Northern Lights, creating a surreal backdrop for winter sports. Imagine gliding down the slopes under the dancing auroras, an experience that will stay with you forever.

Cross-Country Skiing:

Cross-country skiing, or Nordic skiing, is deeply ingrained in Norwegian culture and is a fantastic way to explore the country's winter landscapes. With an extensive network of cross-country trails, known as "løype," Norway offers boundless opportunities for skiers of all levels to traverse its pristine snowy forests and serene wilderness.

Après-Ski and Cosy Cabins:

After an exhilarating day on the slopes, Norway's après-ski scene awaits. Cozy mountain lodges and chalets offer a warm retreat, where you can indulge in traditional Norwegian cuisine and unwind by the fireplace. Embrace the hygge (cozy) atmosphere as you share stories of your adventures with fellow travelers.

Tips for Skiing and Snowboarding in Norway:

1. Weather and Clothing: Norway's winter weather can be unpredictable, so dress in layers and bring waterproof and windproof clothing. Don't forget warm accessories like gloves, hats, and scarves.

2. Daylight Hours: In northern regions, daylight hours during winter can be limited, so plan your activities accordingly. Be sure to bring a headlamp or flashlight for any late afternoon or evening excursions.

3. Skiing Equipment: If you don't have your own skiing or snowboarding gear, most resorts offer equipment rental services. It's advisable to book in advance, especially during peak season.

4. Safety: Always adhere to safety guidelines, follow the resort's rules, and stay within your skill level. If

you're skiing off-piste, ensure you have the necessary equipment and knowledge of avalanche safety.

Whether you're a seasoned skier or a first-time snowboarder, Norway's winter wonderland beckons with its pristine slopes, breathtaking scenery, and warm hospitality. Embrace the thrill of the mountains and immerse yourself in the magic of a skiing and snowboarding experience in Norway – a truly unforgettable winter adventure.

10.3 Wildlife Safaris and Whale Watching

Embark on a thrilling wildlife safari in Norway, where nature's wonders unfold before your eyes in the untamed wilderness. From encountering majestic marine mammals to witnessing elusive Arctic wildlife, the country offers a myriad of opportunities to connect with the animal kingdom like never before.

Whale Watching:
Norway's coastal waters are a playground for whales, and avid whale watchers flock here to witness these gentle giants in their natural habitat. The prime time for whale watching in Norway is from late autumn to early spring when herring and other fish migrate to the Norwegian coast,

attracting whales looking for abundant feeding grounds.

One of the most sought-after species is the magnificent orca, also known as killer whales. The waters around Tromsø, Lofoten Islands, and Vesterålen are renowned for orca sightings during the winter months. Imagine the awe-inspiring moment when a pod of orcas gracefully glides through the Arctic waters, their black and white markings creating a mesmerizing spectacle.

Humpback whales are another common sight during Norway's whale watching season. These acrobatic creatures showcase their impressive breaching and tail-slapping behaviors, leaving visitors in awe of their grace and power. Additionally, minke whales, sperm whales, and pilot whales can also be spotted, adding to the diverse array of marine life encounters.

To enhance the experience, many whale watching tours in Norway are led by expert guides and marine biologists who provide insightful information about these magnificent creatures and the marine ecosystem. These tours prioritize responsible and sustainable practices to ensure minimal disturbance to the whales and their environment.

Arctic Wildlife Safaris:
Beyond whales, Norway's Arctic region is a haven for an array of captivating wildlife. When venturing into the pristine Arctic wilderness, keep your eyes peeled for Arctic foxes, reindeer, and the elusive polar bear, often spotted on the Svalbard archipelago. Svalbard also offers the unique chance to observe nesting seabird colonies, including puffins, guillemots, and kittiwakes, filling the skies with their lively chatter.

For birdwatchers, Norway's coastline hosts a rich variety of avian life. Majestic sea eagles soar through the skies, while colorful puffins dart in and out of their cliffside nests during the summer breeding season.

Nature enthusiasts seeking a more intimate encounter can explore Norway's national parks, such as Dovrefjell-Sunndalsfjella, where wild reindeer roam freely, and musk oxen graze in the rugged terrain.

Tips for Wildlife Safaris and Whale Watching:

- Dress warmly and in layers, as weather conditions can be unpredictable, especially in the Arctic regions.
- Bring binoculars and a camera to capture these incredible moments.
- Listen to and follow the instructions of your knowledgeable guides to ensure a safe and respectful experience for both wildlife and visitors.
- Choose reputable tour operators that prioritize ethical wildlife encounters and sustainability.

Embarking on a wildlife safari and whale watching adventure in Norway provides an extraordinary opportunity to witness some of the Earth's most captivating creatures in their natural habitat. With a commitment to responsible tourism and a wealth of unforgettable encounters, Norway is a dream destination for wildlife enthusiasts and nature lovers alike.

10.4 Camping and Outdoor Activities for Families

Norway's unspoiled wilderness and abundance of outdoor activities make it an ideal destination for families seeking an adventurous and memorable vacation. From camping under the Midnight Sun to embarking on family-friendly hikes, Norway offers a plethora of outdoor experiences that will delight both parents and children alike.

1. Camping in Nature's Embrace:
Camping in Norway is a magical experience, allowing families to immerse themselves in the pristine beauty of the country's landscapes. The right to access and camp on uncultivated land, known as "allemannsretten" or the "Right to Roam," is protected by law, granting families the freedom to pitch their tents in the heart of nature. Whether you prefer camping near a serene fjord, by a glistening lake, or amidst the lush forests, Norway offers endless options for a tranquil retreat.

2. Family-Friendly Hiking Trails:
Norway's hiking trails cater to all ages and skill levels, making it easy for families to explore the great outdoors together. Many trails are well-marked and feature gradual inclines, making them accessible to young children. Popular family-friendly hikes include the Pulpit Rock (Preikestolen) near Stavanger, where you can enjoy breathtaking views from a flat mountain plateau, and the Romsdalseggen Ridge in Åndalsnes, which offers an exciting adventure for older kids.

3. Exploring the Fjords:

A trip to Norway wouldn't be complete without exploring its iconic fjords. Take your family on a fjord cruise to witness the towering cliffs and cascading waterfalls up close. The Nærøyfjord, a UNESCO World Heritage Site, and the Geirangerfjord are particularly popular choices for family-friendly cruises. Kids will be captivated by the stunning natural scenery, and the whole family can enjoy spotting wildlife like seals and eagles along the way.

4. Wildlife Safaris:
Embark on thrilling wildlife safaris to encounter Norway's diverse animal inhabitants. In the northern regions, families can join whale-watching tours to catch a glimpse of majestic orcas and humpback whales swimming in the Arctic waters. For a chance to observe reindeer and the elusive Arctic fox, consider exploring the vast wilderness of Norway's national parks like Dovrefjell-Sunndalsfjella.

5. Thrills on the Water:
Norway's extensive coastline and countless lakes offer endless opportunities for water-based fun. Families can try kayaking, canoeing, or paddleboarding, exploring the serene waters at their own pace. For an adrenaline rush, white-water

rafting adventures are available in certain regions, providing an exciting bonding experience for the whole family.

6. Cycling Adventures:
Hop on a family bike ride and explore Norway's picturesque countryside and charming villages. The country's well-maintained cycle paths offer safe and enjoyable routes for cyclists of all ages. From leisurely rides through scenic valleys to more challenging mountain biking trails, there are options to suit every family's preferences.

7. Outdoor Cooking and Campfires:
A camping trip in Norway isn't complete without cooking meals over an open campfire. Families can bond over preparing traditional Norwegian dishes like "pinnekjøtt" (dried lamb ribs) or roasting marshmallows for a sweet treat. Share stories and create lasting memories as you sit around the warm glow of the campfire beneath the starlit sky.

In Norway, the great outdoors beckons families to embark on extraordinary adventures together, fostering a deeper appreciation for nature and creating cherished memories that will last a lifetime. Whether you're camping by a fjord, hiking through the mountains, or exploring the wildlife-rich landscapes, Norway offers an unparalleled family-friendly experience for nature-loving travelers.

Chapter 11. Safety and Travel Tips

11.1 Emergency Numbers and Services

While Norway is a safe and welcoming destination, it's always essential to be prepared for any unforeseen circumstances during your travels. Familiarizing yourself with emergency numbers and available services is crucial for ensuring your well-being and prompt assistance when needed. Here are the important emergency numbers and services in Norway:

1. Emergency Number: 112

The universal emergency number in Norway, as in many European countries, is 112. This number connects you to police, fire services, and medical assistance. It is free to call from any phone, including landlines, mobile phones, and public payphones.

2. Medical Emergencies:

In the event of a medical emergency, call 113. This number connects you to the emergency medical services (ambulance). The Norwegian emergency medical services are well-equipped and responsive, providing prompt and professional care to those in need.

3. Police:

To report a crime, contact the police by dialing 112. Norway's police force is efficient and reliable, and they are trained to handle various situations, ensuring the safety and security of both residents and visitors.

4. Fire and Rescue Services:

If you encounter a fire or require immediate assistance due to any fire-related incident, call 112. Norway's fire and rescue services are well-trained and equipped to respond swiftly to emergencies and prevent further damages.

5. Sea and Coastal Emergencies:

If you are near or on the coast and require maritime assistance, call the Norwegian Sea Rescue at 120. They specialize in search and rescue operations at sea and along the coast, providing vital assistance in maritime emergencies.

6. Mountain Rescue:

For emergencies in mountainous areas or during outdoor activities in remote regions, dial 112 and ask for mountain rescue assistance. Norway's mountain rescue teams are highly skilled and experienced in handling incidents in challenging terrains.

7. Poison Control Center:

In case of accidental poisoning or related emergencies, contact the Poison Control Center at 22 59 13 00. The center provides expert advice and guidance in cases of poisoning, ingestion of harmful substances, or accidental exposure to toxic materials.

8. European Emergency Number (EU-wide):

If you're an EU resident or a traveler from a country within the European Union, you can also dial 112 for emergency assistance. This number will connect you to the appropriate emergency services in Norway or any EU member state.

Remember that emergency service operators in Norway usually speak English, so don't hesitate to call for help if you find yourself in a critical situation. Keep in mind that Norway's emergency response system is efficient, and responders are trained to handle diverse situations with professionalism and compassion.

Before your trip, it's advisable to store these emergency numbers in your phone and share them with your travel companions. Additionally, check with your travel insurance provider about coverage in case of medical emergencies or other unforeseen events during your stay in Norway. Being prepared and having knowledge of emergency services will ensure you have a safe and enjoyable experience in this beautiful country.

11.2 Safety Guidelines for Families

Norway is a remarkably safe and family-friendly destination, offering a secure environment for travelers of all ages. However, as with any travel, it's essential to take certain precautions to ensure a smooth and worry-free journey. Here are some safety guidelines for families traveling to Norway:

1. Emergency Numbers and Services:
Familiarize yourself with Norway's emergency contact numbers, which are 112 for all emergencies and 113 for medical assistance. Keep your mobile phones charged and accessible at all times. Norway has a well-developed emergency response system, so don't hesitate to call for help if needed.

2. Dressing for the Weather:
Norwegian weather can be unpredictable, even in the summer, so it's vital to dress appropriately for varying conditions. Bring layers of clothing that can be added or removed as needed, along with waterproof and windproof outerwear. Comfortable

footwear is essential, especially if you plan to explore nature trails or fjords.

3. Stay Hydrated and Sun Protection:
During the summer months, especially in the northern regions, the sun can be intense, and it may be easy to get dehydrated. Carry a reusable water bottle and make sure to drink plenty of water, especially when engaging in outdoor activities. Don't forget to apply sunscreen and wear sunglasses and hats to protect from the sun's rays.

4. Follow Local Rules and Safety Signage:
Norway takes safety seriously, and you'll find safety signs and rules in various tourist areas. Pay attention to warning signs near cliffs, waterfalls, and hiking trails. Respect all guidelines, and never venture into restricted or unsafe areas, particularly when traveling with children.

5. Water Safety:
Norway's numerous lakes, fjords, and coastal areas offer beautiful spots for swimming and water-based activities. However, be cautious when swimming, especially in cold waters, and keep a close eye on children at all times. Use designated swimming areas and follow any posted safety instructions.

6. Road Safety:
Norway's road network is generally well-maintained and safe, but be aware of potential hazards, such as narrow and winding mountain roads. Always wear seatbelts, and ensure children are securely buckled in appropriate child seats. Familiarize yourself with Norwegian traffic rules, including speed limits and priority rules.

7. Wildlife Encounters:
Encounters with wildlife can be a memorable experience, but remember to keep a safe distance and never feed wild animals. Norway is home to some large mammals, like moose and reindeer, and seeing them in their natural habitat is a privilege. However, always maintain a respectful distance to avoid any potential dangers.

8. Child-Friendly Facilities:
Norway is an excellent destination for families, and you'll find child-friendly facilities in many places, including restaurants, museums, and accommodation. Look for accommodations with family rooms and amenities catering to children's needs.

9. Personal Belongings:

Keep an eye on your belongings, especially in crowded tourist areas. Petty theft is rare in Norway, but it's always wise to be cautious and use hotel safes or secure locks for valuable items.

10. Medical Considerations:
Ensure that everyone in the family has appropriate medical insurance for the duration of your trip. Norway has an excellent healthcare system, but medical expenses can be costly for non-residents without insurance coverage.

By following these safety guidelines, families can fully embrace the wonders of Norway with peace of mind, creating cherished memories of a safe and enjoyable journey. Always prioritize safety, and let the adventure of exploring Norway's natural beauty and cultural treasures unfold.

11.3 Responsible Travel and Environmental Awareness

As you embark on your journey to Norway, it is essential to approach your travel with a sense of responsibility and environmental awareness. Norway's pristine natural beauty and delicate ecosystems deserve our utmost care and respect. By adopting sustainable practices and being mindful of the impact we have on the environment, we can ensure that this magnificent country remains an enchanting destination for generations to come.

1. Preserve the Wilderness:
Norway's landscapes are a treasure trove of unspoiled wilderness. When exploring the great outdoors, follow designated trails and paths to minimize your impact on the delicate flora and fauna. Refrain from picking wildflowers or disturbing wildlife, and always adhere to the "Leave No Trace" principles, taking your trash with you and leaving nature as you found it.

2. Sustainable Transportation:
Norway offers an efficient and eco-friendly public transportation system, including trains, buses, and ferries. Opt for public transportation whenever possible, as it reduces carbon emissions and helps preserve the natural beauty of the countryside. Additionally, consider walking or cycling through cities and scenic areas to enjoy a more sustainable and immersive experience.

3. Support Eco-Friendly Accommodations:
Choose eco-friendly accommodations that implement sustainable practices and minimize their environmental impact. Many hotels in Norway have adopted green initiatives, such as energy-efficient

lighting, recycling programs, and responsible water usage. Staying in eco-conscious lodgings helps contribute to a greener tourism industry.

4. Conserve Water and Energy:
Norway is known for its abundant fresh water sources, but it's still essential to conserve this precious resource. Take shorter showers, turn off lights and electronics when not in use, and close windows and doors to preserve heat during colder months. Small actions can collectively make a significant difference in reducing energy consumption.

5. Embrace Responsible Wildlife Encounters:
Norway is home to a diverse array of wildlife, including reindeer, whales, and seabirds. When observing wildlife, maintain a respectful distance to avoid causing stress or disruption to their natural behavior. Support tour operators that prioritize ethical wildlife encounters, ensuring the animals' welfare comes first.

6. Reduce Single-Use Plastics:
Norway is actively working to reduce single-use plastics, and you can contribute to this effort by carrying a reusable water bottle, coffee cup, and shopping bag during your travels. Many cities and

towns offer water fountains with potable water, making it easy to refill your bottle.

7. Responsible Fishing and Seafood Consumption:
Norway has a strong fishing tradition, and seafood is a significant part of the cuisine. If you enjoy seafood, choose sustainable options and support fisheries that adhere to responsible fishing practices. Look for eco-label certifications like the Marine Stewardship Council (MSC) when purchasing seafood products.

8. Respect Local Customs and Cultures:
Show respect for Norway's cultural heritage and customs. Familiarize yourself with local traditions, and be mindful of cultural sensitivities when interacting with locals. Engaging in cultural experiences with an open mind fosters cross-cultural understanding and appreciation.

By embracing responsible travel and environmental awareness, you can contribute positively to Norway's preservation while enjoying an enriching and sustainable experience. Let your journey through Norway be a testament to your commitment to protecting the planet and leaving a positive impact on the destinations you explore. Together, we can safeguard the beauty of this remarkable country for future generations to cherish and enjoy.

Chapter 12. Language and Communication

12.1 Common Norwegian Phrases for Travelers

As you embark on your adventure in Norway, embracing some basic Norwegian phrases will undoubtedly enhance your travel experience and foster meaningful connections with the locals. Although English is widely spoken throughout the country, making an effort to speak a few Norwegian words will be appreciated and can make your interactions more enjoyable. Here are some common Norwegian phrases for travelers:

1. Hello / Hi - Hei (pronounced "hey")
2. Good morning - God morgen
3. Good day / Good afternoon - God dag
4. Good evening - God kveld
5. Goodbye - Ha det (informal) / Ha det bra (formal)
6. Yes - Ja
7. No - Nei
8. Please - Vær så snill
9. Thank you - Takk
10. You're welcome - Vær så god
11. Excuse me / Sorry - Unnskyld
12. I don't understand - Jeg forstår ikke
13. Do you speak English? - Snakker du engelsk?

14. My name is... - Mitt navn er...
15. How much is this? - Hvor mye koster dette?
16. Where is...? - Hvor er...?
17. Bathroom / Restroom - Toalett / Bad
18. Help! - Hjelp!
19. Cheers! - Skål!
20. Can I have the menu, please? - Kan jeg få menyen, vær så snill?
21. I love Norway - Jeg elsker Norge
22. What's your name? - Hva heter du?
23. Nice to meet you - Hyggelig å møte deg
24. Can you recommend a good restaurant? - Kan du anbefale en god restaurant?
25. How do I get to...? - Hvordan kommer jeg til...?

Remember, Norwegians are known for their excellent English skills, so don't hesitate to use English if you need help or have a more complex conversation. However, attempting some Norwegian phrases shows respect for the local culture and can lead to delightful exchanges with friendly locals.

Take note that there are different dialects across Norway, and some phrases may vary slightly from one region to another. However, the above phrases are generally understood and used throughout the country. So, embrace the opportunity to engage with Norway's warm and welcoming culture, and savor the unique experiences that await you on your Norwegian journey.

12.2 English Language Availability

For travelers visiting Norway, communication is rarely a barrier, as English language availability is widespread throughout the country. Norwegian society places great emphasis on learning English as a second language, and as a result, most Norwegians, especially in urban areas and tourist destinations, are proficient English speakers.

English as a Second Language:
English is introduced early in the Norwegian education system, and students typically start learning it as a mandatory subject from a young age. This focus on English language education ensures that many Norwegians become fluent speakers by the time they reach adulthood. As a result, you will find that a significant portion of the population, especially the younger generation, can communicate comfortably in English.

Tourism and Hospitality Industry:
Given Norway's popularity as a tourist destination, the tourism and hospitality industry places a strong emphasis on English language proficiency. In

hotels, restaurants, museums, and other tourist-oriented establishments, it is common to encounter staff members who speak fluent English and are able to assist travelers with their needs and inquiries.

Signage and Information:
In major cities and tourist hotspots, important signage, transportation information, and directions are often available in both Norwegian and English. This accommodation makes it easier for international visitors to navigate and enjoy their stay in Norway.

English Language Media and Entertainment:
English-language media, such as newspapers, magazines, and websites, is readily available in Norway. Many popular international television shows and movies are also shown in their original English language, with Norwegian subtitles.

Interactions with Locals:
Travelers will generally find that Norwegians are open and welcoming when approached in English. While some older generations may be less fluent, they are often appreciative of efforts made by visitors to speak English and will still do their best to communicate.

Language Assistance Apps and Tools:
For added convenience, various language translation apps and tools are available for travelers to use on their smartphones. These can assist with translating text, signs, or even conversations in real-time, making it easier to interact and get around.

Overall, English language availability in Norway is excellent, making it a comfortable and accessible destination for travelers from English-speaking countries and other non-Norwegian-speaking countries alike. So, whether you're exploring the vibrant cityscapes or venturing into the serene wilderness, rest assured that the language barrier is likely to be minimal, allowing you to fully immerse yourself in the wonders of Norway.

Chapter 13. Traveling with Kids

13.1 Kid-Friendly Accommodations

When traveling with kids, finding suitable accommodations is essential to ensure a comfortable and enjoyable family vacation. Luckily, Norway caters to families with a range of kid-friendly lodging options that provide the necessary amenities and services to keep both parents and children happy. From cozy cabins in the mountains to family-oriented hotels in the cities, Norway has something for everyone.

1. Family-Friendly Resorts:
Norway boasts several family-friendly resorts that offer a plethora of activities and facilities tailored to children. These resorts often feature on-site playgrounds, swimming pools, and kids' clubs to keep the little ones entertained. Parents can also take advantage of spa facilities, restaurants, and outdoor sports while knowing their kids are well taken care of.

Suggested Resort: Beitostølen Resort - Located in the charming village of Beitostølen, this resort offers a range of family-friendly accommodations, from comfortable cabins to well-appointed apartments. The resort's "Bekkis Baby Club" is perfect for families with infants, while older kids can enjoy activities like horseback riding, cycling, and hiking in the surrounding mountains.

2. Family Suites in Hotels:
Many hotels in Norway offer family suites or interconnected rooms that provide ample space and privacy for families. These suites are equipped with kid-friendly amenities like cribs, baby-changing facilities, and often include additional perks such as children's TV channels and kids' menus in the restaurants.

Suggested Hotel: Thon Hotel Rosenkrantz Oslo - This centrally located hotel in Oslo offers family suites with separate living and sleeping areas, making it a comfortable choice for families. Children will enjoy the complimentary breakfast buffet, and the hotel's central location allows easy access to nearby attractions.

3. Farm Stays:
For a unique and immersive experience, consider staying at a traditional Norwegian farm. Farm stays offer kids a chance to interact with animals, participate in farm activities, and experience the rural way of life. Many farms also provide

home-cooked meals using locally sourced ingredients.

Suggested Farm Stay: Vestre Kjærnes Gård - Situated in the scenic countryside of Vestfold, this farm stay offers charming accommodation in traditional buildings with modern comforts. Kids will love feeding the animals, exploring the farm, and engaging in outdoor activities.

4. Family-Friendly Cabins:
For families seeking a rustic escape surrounded by nature, renting a cabin can be an excellent choice. Cabins often come equipped with kitchens, allowing parents to prepare meals for picky eaters, and offer plenty of space for kids to play outdoors.

Suggested Cabin Rental: Geilo - Geilo is a popular ski resort town that transforms into a family-friendly destination during the summer months. Renting a cabin here allows families to explore the stunning landscapes, enjoy outdoor activities like hiking and biking, and experience the laid-back Norwegian lifestyle.

When booking kid-friendly accommodations in Norway, it's essential to consider the location and nearby attractions that cater to children's interests.

Whether you opt for a resort with comprehensive facilities or a cozy cabin tucked away in the wilderness, Norway's kid-friendly accommodations ensure that the whole family will cherish their Norwegian adventure for years to come.

13.2 Packing Essentials for Children

Traveling to Norway with children presents a wonderful opportunity for families to explore the country's captivating landscapes and immerse themselves in its vibrant culture. However, packing for little ones requires some extra thought and preparation to ensure their comfort and safety throughout the journey. Here's a list of essential items to pack when traveling to Norway with children:

1. Weather-Appropriate Clothing:
Norwegian weather can be quite unpredictable, so it's essential to pack a variety of clothing suitable for different conditions. Layering is key, as temperatures can fluctuate throughout the day. Be sure to include:
   - Warm, waterproof winter jackets and snowsuits for colder months.
   - Lightweight, breathable raincoats and waterproof pants for the wetter seasons.

- Insulated, moisture-wicking base layers to keep children comfortable during outdoor activities.
- Hats, scarves, and gloves to protect against the chilly winds.

2. Sturdy Footwear:
Ensure your children have comfortable and sturdy footwear appropriate for the activities you have planned. Waterproof boots with good traction are ideal for exploring nature trails, hiking in the mountains, or splashing around in puddles.

3. Sun Protection:
Even during the colder months, the sun can be quite strong, especially in snowy areas. Pack sunscreen with a high SPF, sunglasses, and wide-brimmed hats to protect your little ones' skin and eyes from harmful UV rays.

4. Insect Repellent:
In the summer months, particularly in forested areas or near water bodies, mosquitoes and other insects can be bothersome. Bring insect repellent to keep those pesky bugs at bay and ensure a more enjoyable outdoor experience.

5. Medications and First Aid Kit:

Carry any necessary medications your children may need during the trip. Also, pack a basic first aid kit containing band-aids, antiseptic wipes, pain relievers, and any essential medical supplies for minor injuries or illnesses.

6. Travel Documents and Identification:
Don't forget your children's passports or identification cards if required for the trip. It's also a good idea to have a copy of their health insurance information and emergency contact details.

7. Travel Entertainment:
Long journeys and waiting times can be challenging for children, so pack some travel entertainment to keep them occupied. Consider bringing their favorite books, toys, coloring books, puzzles, or electronic devices loaded with games or movies.

8. Snacks and Hydration:
Pack some healthy snacks that your children enjoy to keep hunger at bay while on the go. Also, carry refillable water bottles to ensure they stay hydrated, especially during active outdoor adventures.

9. Diapers and Baby Supplies:
If you're traveling with infants or toddlers, pack an ample supply of diapers, wipes, and other necessary

baby items. While Norway offers baby care products, having your preferred brands can provide added convenience.

10. Language and Communication Aids:
Bring a pocket-sized phrasebook or language translation app to help with communication, especially if you're traveling to more remote areas where English may not be as widely spoken.

By packing these essential items, you can ensure a stress-free and enjoyable adventure for your children in Norway. With their comfort taken care of, your family can focus on creating lasting memories amidst Norway's stunning landscapes and warm-hearted communities.

13.3 Childcare Services and Facilities

Traveling with children can be a rewarding and enriching experience, and Norway is a family-friendly destination that caters well to the needs of parents and their little ones. The country offers a range of childcare services and facilities that ensure both parents and children can enjoy their vacation with ease and peace of mind.

1. Kindergartens and Daycare Centers:

Norway is known for its excellent childcare system, and many cities and towns have well-established kindergartens and daycare centers. These institutions offer a safe and nurturing environment for children to play and interact with others their age. While these services are primarily designed for Norwegian residents, some larger cities may have international daycare centers that can accommodate short-term visitors.

2. Family-Friendly Accommodations:
Hotels, guesthouses, and resorts in Norway often cater to families traveling with children. Many establishments provide family rooms with extra space and amenities to accommodate parents and kids comfortably. Look for hotels that offer cribs, extra beds, or connecting rooms to suit your family's needs.

3. Child-Friendly Restaurants and Menus:
Norwegian restaurants are generally welcoming to families, and many eateries offer child-friendly menus with simplified dishes and portion sizes. High chairs are commonly available in most restaurants, making mealtime hassle-free for parents with young children.

4. Public Facilities and Changing Stations:

Public facilities in Norway are equipped with amenities for families. You'll find changing tables in most restrooms, both in urban areas and popular tourist spots. These well-maintained facilities ensure that parents can take care of their children's needs conveniently while exploring the country.

5. Outdoor Playgrounds and Parks:
Norway boasts an abundance of outdoor spaces and playgrounds where kids can run, play, and burn off their energy. Public parks and recreational areas in cities and towns often have well-designed play structures, swings, and slides, providing an excellent opportunity for children to socialize and have fun.

6. Child-Friendly Attractions and Museums:
Many attractions and museums in Norway are family-friendly, offering interactive exhibits and activities suitable for children. From science centers to open-air museums and wildlife parks, these venues ensure that kids have a memorable and educational experience during their visit.

7. Childcare Services for Tourists:
In some tourist destinations, especially during peak seasons, you may find specialized childcare services offered to travelers. These services may include

temporary babysitting options or organized group activities for children, allowing parents to enjoy some adult time while their kids are well taken care of.

8. Baby Supplies and Stores:
Major cities in Norway have a wide range of stores and supermarkets where you can purchase baby supplies such as diapers, baby food, and formula. Pharmacies (apotek) also carry essential baby care items if needed.

Remember that Norway values family life, and it's not uncommon to see parents with young children in various public spaces. Norwegian society is generally accommodating and understanding of families' needs, making it a welcoming destination for travelers with kids.

While planning your trip to Norway, ensure that you have the necessary documents and arrangements for your child's travel, including travel insurance that covers any unforeseen circumstances. With childcare services and facilities readily available, you can focus on creating cherished memories with your family as you explore the wonders of Norway together.

13.4 Tips for Keeping Kids Engaged During Travel

1. Involve Kids in Planning:
Before your trip, include your kids in the travel planning process. Show them pictures and videos of Norway's attractions, fjords, and wildlife to spark their excitement and curiosity. Discuss potential activities and let them choose some destinations or experiences they would like to explore. By involving them from the start, they'll feel more invested in the journey.

2. Storytelling and Legends:
Norwegian folklore is filled with captivating stories of trolls, mythical creatures, and brave Vikings. Share these fascinating tales with your children to spark their imagination and create a sense of wonder about the places you'll visit. Encourage them to come up with their own stories or draw pictures inspired by these legends during downtime.

3. Wildlife Spotting:
Norway's diverse landscapes are home to a variety of wildlife, including reindeer, whales, puffins, and arctic foxes. Engage your kids in wildlife spotting activities during your travels. Go on wildlife safaris, visit animal parks, or take whale watching tours

where they can witness these beautiful creatures in their natural habitats.

4. Nature Exploration and Scavenger Hunts:
Norway's outdoors offer endless opportunities for exploration. Organize nature scavenger hunts, where kids can search for specific plants, rocks, or wildlife while hiking in the woods or by the fjords. Provide them with binoculars and magnifying glasses to observe nature up close.

5. Hands-On Museums and Interactive Exhibits:
Norway is home to several interactive museums and science centers that are perfect for engaging young minds. Oslo's Viking Ship Museum, Bergen's VilVite Science Center, and Trondheim's Vitensenteret are just a few examples. Let your kids participate in hands-on exhibits and educational activities that make learning fun.

6. Cultural Workshops:
Introduce your kids to Norwegian culture through workshops and craft activities. Many cities offer workshops where kids can learn traditional crafts like rosemaling (decorative painting), making wooden trolls, or crafting their own Viking shields. These experiences will create lasting memories and a deeper connection to Norwegian heritage.

7. Kid-Friendly Tours and Activities:
Look for family-oriented tours and activities tailored to children. From boat rides along the fjords to guided nature walks, there are plenty of excursions designed with kids in mind. Local guides can often make history and culture come alive in an engaging and age-appropriate way.

8. Visit Kid-Friendly Attractions:
Plan visits to attractions specifically designed for kids. Amusement parks like TusenFryd near Oslo or the Flor & Fjære garden on Sør-Hidle Island offer family-friendly entertainment. Zoos, aquariums, and wildlife parks are also popular choices for children.

9. Embrace Outdoor Play:
Norway's outdoor playground is vast and inviting. Let your kids run, play, and explore in the open spaces. Many cities have well-maintained parks with playgrounds where they can burn off energy and make new friends with local children.

10. Emphasize Norway's Mythical Creatures:
Norwegian folklore is full of intriguing mythical creatures like trolls and hulders. Encourage kids to look out for troll statues or hulder-inspired art

during your travels. Engage in discussions about these legendary beings, igniting their sense of curiosity and imagination.

By incorporating these engaging activities and experiences into your family's itinerary, your children will not only have a fantastic time in Norway but will also develop a deeper appreciation for the country's natural beauty, culture, and folklore. Norway's enchanting landscapes and rich history are sure to leave a lasting impression on the young adventurers' hearts.

Chapter 14. Traveling as a Couple

14.1 Romantic Accommodations and Packages

Norway's enchanting landscapes and serene beauty create the perfect backdrop for romantic getaways, making it an idyllic destination for couples seeking to kindle or celebrate their love. From secluded cabins nestled in the wilderness to luxurious hotels offering panoramic views of the fjords, Norway presents a plethora of romantic accommodations and packages to create cherished memories with your loved one.

1. Luxury Fjord-side Retreats:
Indulge in the ultimate romantic experience by staying at one of Norway's luxury fjord-side retreats. Imagine waking up to the sight of majestic fjords stretching before you, with mountains rising in the background. These exclusive retreats often offer private balconies, spa facilities, and gourmet dining experiences. Treat yourselves to couples' massages, enjoy a candlelit dinner with stunning fjord views, and immerse yourselves in the tranquility of nature.

Suggestion: Solstrand Hotel & Bad (Bergen): This historic hotel exudes old-world charm and is beautifully located on the shores of the Bjørnefjorden. With its classic architecture, serene surroundings, and top-notch amenities, it offers a dreamy escape for couples.

2. Cozy Cabins in the Arctic:
For an intimate and secluded experience, head to the Arctic regions of Norway and retreat to cozy cabins surrounded by snow-capped mountains and pristine wilderness. These cabins often come equipped with private saunas and hot tubs, providing the perfect setting for stargazing or witnessing the mesmerizing Northern Lights together.

Suggestion: Lyngen Lodge (Lyngen Alps): This remote lodge offers panoramic views of the Lyngenfjord and is an ideal base for exploring the Arctic wonders. With its welcoming atmosphere, log cabins, and outdoor activities, it's a haven for couples seeking an Arctic romance.

3. Romantic City Escapes:
Norway's cities have their fair share of romantic accommodations, perfect for couples who desire a blend of urban charm and cultural experiences. Stay in boutique hotels with stylish interiors and convenient city-center locations, allowing you to

explore museums, art galleries, and quaint streets hand in hand.

Suggestion: The Thief (Oslo): This chic and contemporary hotel located on Tjuvholmen Island offers a blend of modern luxury and art-focused design. It's a stone's throw away from museums like the Astrup Fearnley and offers breathtaking views of the Oslofjord.

Romantic Packages:
Many hotels and lodges in Norway offer special romantic packages designed to make your stay even more memorable. These packages often include extras such as champagne on arrival, candlelit dinners, spa treatments, and guided romantic activities.

Suggestion: Arctic Romance Package at Sorrisniva Igloo Hotel (Alta): Experience a unique Arctic romance at this ice hotel with the Arctic Romance Package. Enjoy a night in a cozy ice room, followed by a traditional Sami dinner in a lavvu (Sami tent) with a roaring fire and Northern Lights gazing.

No matter the season, Norway's romantic accommodations and packages promise to ignite the sparks of love and create cherished moments that will be etched in your hearts forever. Whether you prefer secluded escapes in the Arctic wilderness or luxurious indulgence overlooking the fjords, Norway invites you to embark on a romantic journey filled with shared wonders and unforgettable experiences.

14.2 *Couples' Activities and Itineraries*

Norway's stunning landscapes, enchanting cities, and romantic atmosphere make it an ideal destination for couples seeking a memorable and intimate getaway. Whether you're newlyweds on your honeymoon, celebrating an anniversary, or simply looking to rekindle your love amid breathtaking scenery, Norway offers a plethora of romantic experiences that will leave you with cherished memories to last a lifetime. Here are some handpicked couples' activities and itineraries to make the most of your time in Norway:

Romantic Fjord Cruises:
Embark on a romantic journey through Norway's iconic fjords hand in hand with your loved one. Take a cruise through the serene waters of Geirangerfjord, Nærøyfjord, or the UNESCO-listed Sognefjord, where majestic cliffs rise from the deep blue waters, and cascading waterfalls create a dreamlike setting. Relax on deck as you soak in the

natural splendor, or cozy up in the warmth of the ship's lounge, savoring the breathtaking views from the comfort of your seat.

Magical Northern Lights Hunts:
If you're visiting Norway during the winter months, witnessing the Northern Lights together is a magical and awe-inspiring experience. Head to the Arctic regions, such as Tromsø or Lofoten, where you can join guided Northern Lights tours. Set out under the Arctic skies, hand in hand, as you wait for the celestial lights to paint the heavens with their mesmerizing colors, creating an unforgettable moment of togetherness under nature's greatest spectacle.

Scenic Train Journeys:
Embark on a romantic train journey through Norway's picturesque landscapes, passing by snow-capped mountains, tranquil lakes, and charming villages. The Flåm Railway, known for its steep ascent and breathtaking views, takes you from the mountains to the fjords, offering opportunities for intimate moments amid Norway's captivating scenery.

Charming Strolls in Coastal Cities:

Explore the charm of Norway's coastal cities hand in hand with leisurely strolls along the waterfronts. Bergen's Bryggen, with its colorful wooden buildings, exudes a quaint and historical ambiance perfect for romantic walks. In Oslo, take a leisurely stroll along Aker Brygge, an inviting waterfront district dotted with cafes and restaurants, creating a delightful atmosphere for couples to unwind and enjoy each other's company.

Cosy Cabins and Retreats:
Escape to one of Norway's remote cabins or lodges for a secluded and romantic retreat. Surrounded by nature's tranquility, these cozy accommodations provide an ideal setting for intimate evenings by the fireplace, stargazing from the outdoor hot tub, and sharing cherished moments in a private, serene environment.

Dining with a View:
Indulge in romantic candlelit dinners with a view in some of Norway's most scenic locations. Choose from restaurants perched on mountaintops, overlooking fjords, or nestled by the seaside. Savor the taste of local delicacies as you savor the picturesque panoramas together.

Itinerary Suggestion - Romantic Escape to Norway:

Day 1: Arrive in Oslo - Explore the city's cultural gems and vibrant atmosphere.
Day 2-3: Take the Flåm Railway to the fjords - Stay in a charming cabin and cruise the fjords.
Day 4-5: Journey to Tromsø - Enjoy Northern Lights hunts and Arctic experiences.
Day 6-7: Head to Bergen - Wander through the city's historic streets and take a fjord cruise.
Day 8: Return to Oslo - Indulge in a romantic farewell dinner.

Norway's romantic allure lies not only in its picturesque landscapes but also in the sense of adventure and togetherness it fosters. Whether you're reveling in the magical Northern Lights, cruising through serene fjords, or simply savoring each other's company in a cozy cabin, Norway promises an enchanting escape for couples seeking love and romance amid nature's grandeur.

14.3 Intimate Date Night Recommendations

Norway's enchanting landscapes and romantic settings make it an ideal destination for couples seeking an intimate and memorable date night experience. Whether you're strolling hand-in-hand through charming city streets or cozying up under the magical Northern Lights, Norway offers a plethora of romantic options to create lasting memories with your loved one. Here are some intimate date night recommendations that will make your time in Norway truly special:

1. Northern Lights Viewing:
Witnessing the ethereal dance of the Northern Lights is a once-in-a-lifetime experience that exudes romance. Head to Tromsø or Lofoten during the winter months for the best chances of catching this natural light show. Bundle up together under a blanket, enjoy a warm cup of cocoa, and marvel at the mesmerizing colors painting the Arctic sky.

2. Fjord Cruise at Sunset:
Embark on a private fjord cruise as the sun begins to set, casting a warm glow over the majestic fjords. Several tour operators offer intimate boat trips with cozy seating arrangements, where you can enjoy each other's company while surrounded by Norway's awe-inspiring scenery. Don't forget to bring along a bottle of champagne to toast to your love amidst nature's grandeur.

3. Candlelit Dinner in Bergen:
The picturesque city of Bergen offers a romantic setting for a candlelit dinner. Enjoy a meal at a waterfront restaurant with views of Bryggen's

historic wooden buildings and the glistening harbor. As the sun sets, the soft glow of candlelight adds an intimate touch to your dining experience.

4. Midnight Sun Picnic:
During the summer months in northern Norway, the Midnight Sun bathes the landscape in an ethereal light, offering endless daylight even at midnight. Pack a picnic basket with local delicacies and find a secluded spot near a tranquil lake or atop a scenic hill. Experience the magic of a romantic picnic under the golden glow of the Midnight Sun.

5. Relaxing Spa Evening:
Indulge in a relaxing spa evening at one of Norway's luxurious wellness retreats. Many hotels and lodges offer spa facilities with saunas, hot tubs, and couples' treatments. Unwind together, enjoying massages or simply soaking in the soothing ambiance while surrounded by Norway's natural beauty.

6. Secluded Cabin Getaway:
Escape the hustle and bustle of city life and retreat to a secluded cabin in the wilderness. Norway is dotted with charming cabins tucked away in the mountains or along the shores of serene lakes. Spend the evening snuggled up by the fireplace,

sharing stories and cherishing each other's company.

7. Stargazing in the Wilderness:
Venture away from city lights and explore Norway's pristine wilderness for a night of stargazing. Lay down a blanket, gaze up at the clear night sky, and admire the stars in all their glory. If you're lucky, you might even spot shooting stars, making your romantic moment even more special.

8. Evening Walk through Oslo's Vigeland Park:
Take a leisurely evening stroll through Vigeland Park in Oslo, a captivating sculpture park with over 200 bronze and granite statues by artist Gustav Vigeland. As the sun sets, the park takes on a magical ambiance, offering an intimate atmosphere for heartfelt conversations and moments of connection.

No matter which corner of Norway you choose for your date night, the country's natural beauty and warm ambiance set the stage for an unforgettable romantic experience. Embrace the magic of Norway and create cherished memories with your loved one in this captivating Nordic wonderland.

Chapter 15. Traveling with Disabilities

15.1 Accessibility Information and Resources

Norway is committed to providing an inclusive and accessible travel experience for all visitors, including those with disabilities. From well-designed infrastructure to dedicated services, the country offers a range of resources to ensure that travelers of varying mobility levels can explore its breathtaking landscapes and vibrant cities comfortably. Here are some essential accessibility information and resources for people traveling with disabilities to Norway:

1. Accessible Transportation:
Norway's transportation system caters to travelers with disabilities. Many public buses, trains, and trams are equipped with facilities for wheelchair users, such as ramps and designated spaces. Additionally, major airports and train stations provide assistance for passengers with reduced mobility, including accessible restrooms and elevators.

2. Accommodation:
Numerous hotels, guesthouses, and cabins throughout Norway are designed with accessibility

in mind. Look for accommodations labeled as "universal design" or "accessible rooms" that feature amenities like wider doorways, roll-in showers, and handrails.

3. Tourist Attractions and Activities:
Several of Norway's popular tourist attractions and landmarks have taken measures to ensure accessibility. Many museums, historical sites, and outdoor destinations offer ramps, elevators, and accessible paths. For instance, many fjord cruises and boat tours are equipped to accommodate wheelchair users.

4. National Parks and Nature Reserves:
Norway's stunning national parks and nature reserves are accessible to people with disabilities, with some areas providing wheelchair-friendly trails and facilities. Additionally, the Norwegian Trekking Association (DNT) offers information on accessible cabins and routes for hikers with reduced mobility.

5. Information Centers:
VisitNorway, the official tourism board, provides comprehensive accessibility information on its website and through tourist information centers. The staff at these centers are knowledgeable about

accessible attractions, transportation options, and can provide tailored advice for travelers with disabilities.

6. Assistance Services:
Norwegian cities offer disability assistance services like "TT-kort," a special card granting free public transport for disabled individuals and their assistants. Some attractions also provide personal assistants for visitors with disabilities upon request.

7. Car Rental and Mobility Equipment:
Several car rental companies in Norway offer adapted vehicles for travelers with disabilities. Additionally, specialized mobility equipment, such as wheelchairs and scooters, can be rented in major cities.

8. Norwegian Sign Language (NSL):
For travelers with hearing impairments, it's worth noting that Norwegian Sign Language is officially recognized in Norway. Some tourist information centers and services may have staff who are proficient in NSL.

9. Online Resources:
Online resources, such as the Accessible Norway website (accessible-norway.no), offer valuable

information on accessible attractions, accommodation, and travel tips for people with disabilities.

10. Planning Ahead:
While Norway endeavors to be inclusive, it's advisable for travelers with disabilities to plan ahead. Contact hotels and attractions in advance to ensure they can accommodate specific needs and preferences. This foresight will help to create a smooth and enjoyable travel experience.

Norway's commitment to accessibility and the seamless integration of travelers with disabilities into its cultural and natural offerings exemplifies the country's progressive outlook. With a wealth of accessible resources and an inviting atmosphere, Norway welcomes all visitors to discover the magic of its breathtaking landscapes and vibrant cultural heritage.

15.2 Adaptive Tours and Activities

Norway is a country that prides itself on its commitment to inclusivity and accessibility, making it a welcoming destination for travelers with disabilities. Whether you're a wheelchair user, have limited mobility, or face other challenges, Norway offers a range of adaptive tours and activities that ensure everyone can experience the country's natural beauty, cultural richness, and thrilling adventures.

1. Accessible Fjord Cruises:
Discover Norway's world-famous fjords in comfort with specially designed accessible cruises. Many operators provide barrier-free access to their vessels, ensuring wheelchair users can navigate the decks and enjoy the breathtaking views of the fjords, glaciers, and cascading waterfalls. Knowledgeable guides often offer audio description services to enhance the experience for visually impaired travelers.

2. Wheelchair-Friendly City Tours:
Explore Norway's charming cities on wheelchair-friendly guided tours. Cities like Oslo, Bergen, and Trondheim offer accessible routes that showcase historical landmarks, cultural attractions, and vibrant cityscapes. Knowledgeable guides will share captivating stories about each city's history and provide insights into Norwegian culture.

3. Inclusive Wildlife Safaris:
Embark on thrilling wildlife safaris tailored for travelers with disabilities. Arctic excursions in the north, such as those in Tromsø or Svalbard, offer

opportunities to witness polar bears, reindeer, and other Arctic animals. Specially equipped vehicles or sledges are available to accommodate wheelchair users, ensuring that no one misses out on these memorable experiences.

4. Adaptive Snow Sports:
During the winter months, Norway's ski resorts offer adaptive snow sports programs for travelers with disabilities. Adaptive skiing, snowboarding, and sit-skiing allow individuals with physical challenges to glide down the slopes alongside their friends and family. Trained instructors and adaptive equipment make these activities safe and enjoyable for all.

5. Accessible Hiking Trails:
Discover the natural wonders of Norway on accessible hiking trails that cater to a range of abilities. Many national parks and nature reserves offer designated routes suitable for wheelchair users and those with limited mobility. Experience the serenity of lush forests, cascading waterfalls, and picturesque landscapes without barriers.

6. Interactive Museums and Cultural Activities:
Norway's museums and cultural centers prioritize accessibility for all visitors. Explore interactive

exhibitions and participate in hands-on activities that engage all senses. Many museums offer audio guides, tactile displays, and Braille materials to enhance the experience for visually impaired visitors.

7. Adaptive Kayaking and Boat Tours:
Take to the tranquil waters of Norway's rivers, lakes, and coastal regions on adaptive kayaking or boat tours. Specially designed kayaks and boats equipped with accessible features allow travelers with disabilities to join in on aquatic adventures and observe the country's diverse marine life and stunning scenery.

8. Thermal Springs and Relaxation:
Experience the therapeutic benefits of Norway's thermal springs and spas, many of which offer accessible facilities for travelers with disabilities. Soak in soothing hot springs, indulge in massages, and unwind amidst the picturesque landscapes that surround these wellness retreats.

9. Inclusive Culinary Experiences:
Partake in Norway's culinary delights with inclusive dining experiences. Many restaurants and food tours cater to individuals with disabilities, offering

accessible seating arrangements and menus that accommodate various dietary needs.

When planning your trip to Norway, it's essential to communicate any specific requirements or needs with tour operators and accommodation providers in advance. Norway's commitment to accessibility ensures that everyone can relish the country's wonders and create lasting memories of an inclusive and unforgettable journey.

15.3 Disability-Friendly Accommodations

Norway is a country that strives to be inclusive and accessible to all travelers, including those with disabilities. Travelers can find a range of disability-friendly accommodations throughout the country, offering accessible facilities and services to ensure a comfortable and enjoyable stay. From modern hotels to charming guesthouses, these accommodations are equipped to cater to the specific needs of individuals with disabilities.

Features of Disability-Friendly Accommodations:
1. Wheelchair Accessibility: Disability-friendly accommodations typically have ramps and elevators to provide easy access to common areas and guestrooms for wheelchair users.

2. Accessible Rooms: These accommodations offer specially designed rooms with wider doorways, spacious bathrooms with grab bars, and other accessibility features to ensure a comfortable stay for guests with disabilities.

3. Supportive Staff: The staff at disability-friendly accommodations are trained to provide assistance and support to guests with disabilities, ensuring their needs are met with care and understanding.

4. Location: Many of these accommodations are conveniently situated near accessible transportation options and attractions, making it easier for travelers with disabilities to explore the surrounding areas.

5. Inclusive Amenities: Disability-friendly accommodations often offer amenities like accessible swimming pools, restaurants, and common areas to ensure all guests can enjoy their stay.

Accommodation Suggestions:

1. Scandic Hotels:
Scandic Hotels is a renowned hotel chain in Norway known for its commitment to accessibility. Many of

their properties offer specially designed rooms and facilities for guests with disabilities. Scandic hotels have wide corridors, accessible entrances, and elevators, making them an excellent choice for travelers with mobility impairments. They also provide amenities such as visual alarms and assistive listening devices for guests with hearing impairments.

2. Thon Hotels:
Thon Hotels is another hotel chain in Norway that places a strong emphasis on accessibility. They offer accessible rooms with spacious layouts, grab bars, and roll-in showers to cater to guests with mobility challenges. Thon Hotels also strive to meet the needs of guests with visual or hearing impairments by providing accessible signage and communication options.

3. Radisson Blu Hotels:
Radisson Blu Hotels in Norway are known for their dedication to inclusivity. These hotels offer accessible rooms with carefully designed bathrooms and supportive facilities. Guests with disabilities can expect attentive service from the staff, who are trained to assist with any specific needs.

Remember to Book in Advance:

While Norway has made great strides in providing disability-friendly accommodations, it is advisable to book your accommodations well in advance, especially during peak travel seasons. This ensures that you secure the most suitable rooms and that the hotel can adequately prepare for your arrival.

Accessible accommodations in Norway not only provide comfort and convenience but also allow travelers with disabilities to fully immerse themselves in the country's natural beauty, cultural treasures, and warm hospitality. By choosing disability-friendly accommodations, you can focus on creating lasting memories during your Norwegian adventure with ease and peace of mind.

Chapter 16. Itinerary Suggestions

16.1 One Week Family Adventure

Norway's diverse landscapes and family-friendly activities make it an ideal destination for an unforgettable one-week adventure with your loved ones. This itinerary highlights some of the country's top attractions and experiences that cater to both children and adults, ensuring a magical and enriching journey for the whole family.

Day 1: Arrival in Oslo
- Arrive in Oslo, the capital city of Norway.
- Check into your family-friendly accommodation.
- Spend the afternoon exploring Oslo's iconic landmarks, such as the Royal Palace, Aker Brygge waterfront, and the Opera House.
- Visit the Vigeland Park, a sprawling sculpture park with over 200 statues, perfect for kids to roam and discover.

Day 2: Family-Friendly Museums
- Begin the day at the Viking Ship Museum, where you can marvel at well-preserved Viking ships and artifacts.
- Head to the Fram Museum to learn about polar exploration and the adventures of Roald Amundsen and Fridtjof Nansen.

- Visit the Kon-Tiki Museum, dedicated to the thrilling expeditions of Thor Heyerdahl.
- After an exciting day of exploration, enjoy a family dinner at one of Oslo's cozy restaurants.

Day 3: Journey to Bergen
- Take a scenic train ride from Oslo to Bergen, one of the most beautiful train journeys in the world.
- Arrive in Bergen and check into your family-friendly accommodation.
- Stroll through the charming streets of Bryggen, a UNESCO World Heritage Site, lined with colorful wooden houses.
- Visit the Bergen Fish Market, where you can sample fresh seafood and local delicacies.

Day 4: Fløibanen and Mount Fløyen
- Take the Fløibanen funicular to the top of Mount Fløyen for breathtaking views of Bergen and its surrounding fjords.
- Enjoy family-friendly activities on Mount Fløyen, such as hiking, playgrounds, and picnics.
- Return to the city and explore the Bergenhus Fortress and Håkon's Hall.

Day 5: Fjord Cruise and Waterfalls

- Embark on a family-friendly fjord cruise from Bergen to explore the stunning Nærøyfjord, a UNESCO World Heritage Site.
- Sail through scenic landscapes, passing waterfalls and quaint villages along the way.
- Enjoy the fresh mountain air and take in the natural beauty of the fjords.
- Return to Bergen in the evening and indulge in a delightful family dinner.

Day 6: Bergen Aquarium and Science Center
- Visit the Bergen Aquarium, a fascinating attraction for kids to learn about marine life, featuring penguins, seals, and fish.
- Head to VilVite, Bergen's science center, offering interactive exhibits and activities that engage young minds.
- Spend the afternoon at Bergen's public parks or enjoying a leisurely boat ride on the city's lakes.

Day 7: Departure from Bergen
- On your final day, explore any remaining attractions or revisit your favorite spots in Bergen.
- Depending on your departure time, you may have a chance to do some last-minute shopping or enjoy a relaxing family meal before bidding farewell to Norway.

This one-week family adventure in Norway captures the essence of the country's natural wonders, historical treasures, and family-oriented attractions. From vibrant cities to majestic fjords, your family will create cherished memories that will last a lifetime. Keep in mind that Norway offers endless possibilities for exploration, so feel free to tailor the itinerary to your family's preferences and interests.

16.2 Romantic Two-Week Getaway

Day 1-3: Oslo - Enchanting Capital City
Arrive in Oslo, Norway's capital, and immerse yourselves in its captivating blend of modernity and history. Spend the first day exploring the iconic landmarks, including the Royal Palace and Oslo Opera House. Stroll hand-in-hand through the charming streets of Aker Brygge, a waterfront district filled with restaurants and boutiques. Visit the Vigeland Park, an enchanting sculpture park with over 200 statues. For a romantic evening, take a sunset cruise on the Oslofjord, savoring stunning views of the city.

Day 4-6: Bergen - A UNESCO World Heritage City
Fly or take a scenic train journey to Bergen, a UNESCO-listed gem surrounded by fjords and mountains. Spend the next few days discovering the

city's historic charm and natural wonders. Take a romantic funicular ride up Mount Fløyen for panoramic views of Bergen and its surroundings. Meander through the Bryggen Hanseatic Wharf, a picturesque area with colorful wooden buildings. Enjoy a romantic seafood dinner by the harbor, savoring freshly caught Norwegian delicacies.

Day 7-9: The Fjords - Serenity Amidst Nature's Grandeur
Embark on an unforgettable journey into the heart of Norway's fjords. Rent a car or join a guided tour to explore the stunning Nærøyfjord and Sognefjord, both UNESCO World Heritage Sites. Experience the tranquility of the fjords as you sail through the dramatic landscapes, passing waterfalls, cliffs, and charming villages. Opt for a secluded cabin stay with views of the fjords, allowing you to relish quiet moments with your loved one.

Day 10-12: Tromsø - Romance Under the Midnight Sun
Fly to Tromsø, known as the "Gateway to the Arctic," and prepare for a magical experience under the Midnight Sun. In summer, Tromsø is bathed in ethereal light, providing the perfect backdrop for romantic adventures. Explore the Arctic Cathedral and take a cable car ride to the Storsteinen

mountain for sweeping vistas. Embrace the Arctic romance by going on a midnight boat tour or hiking in the surrounding wilderness. If visiting during winter, chase the mesmerizing Northern Lights together, adding a touch of enchantment to your journey.

Day 13-14: Lofoten Islands - An Idyllic Escape
Fly or take a short ferry to the captivating Lofoten Islands, a picturesque archipelago renowned for its dramatic scenery. Spend your last days basking in the beauty of pristine beaches, fishing villages, and majestic mountains. Take a leisurely hike together to appreciate the serene surroundings or indulge in a seafood feast at one of the local restaurants. Enjoy each other's company as you savor the idyllic atmosphere of this enchanting destination.

Note: The above itinerary is a suggested outline for a romantic two-week getaway in Norway. Feel free to tailor it to your preferences, adding or omitting destinations based on your interests. Norway's vast landscapes and diverse regions offer endless opportunities for romance and adventure, making it an ideal destination for an unforgettable couple's retreat.

16.3 Multi-Generational Travel Experience

Norway's captivating landscapes and family-friendly attractions make it an ideal destination for multi-generational travel. This itinerary caters to all age groups, offering a delightful blend of outdoor adventures, cultural experiences, and relaxation. From the stunning fjords to the charming cities, this journey will create cherished memories for the whole family.

Day 1: Arrival in Oslo
- Arrive in Oslo, the vibrant capital of Norway.
- Check-in at a family-friendly hotel and rest after your journey.
- Take a leisurely stroll through the city center, visiting landmarks like the Royal Palace and Oslo City Hall.
- Optional: Explore the Norwegian Maritime Museum, perfect for all generations with its interactive exhibits.

Day 2: Discovering Oslo's Museums
- Begin the day at the Viking Ship Museum, where kids and adults alike will be fascinated by ancient artifacts.
- Visit the Fram Museum to learn about polar exploration and the famous ship Fram.

- Head to the Vigeland Park, showcasing over 200 captivating sculptures and offering spacious lawns for picnics and relaxation.
- Enjoy dinner at a family-friendly restaurant with local cuisine options.

Day 3: Journey to Bergen
- Take a scenic train ride from Oslo to Bergen, enjoying picturesque views of the Norwegian countryside.
- Upon arrival in Bergen, explore the UNESCO-listed Bryggen Hanseatic Wharf with its colorful wooden buildings.
- Visit the Bergen Fish Market, where everyone can sample fresh seafood and local delicacies.

Day 4: Exploring Bergen
- Embark on a funicular ride to Mount Fløyen, offering panoramic views of Bergen and the surrounding fjords.
- Visit the Bergen Aquarium, an engaging experience for both kids and adults, featuring a variety of marine life.
- Enjoy a boat tour on the fjords, providing a memorable experience for all generations.

Day 5: Journey to Geiranger

- Take a scenic drive or ferry from Bergen to Geiranger, passing through breathtaking landscapes.
- Arrive in Geiranger, a picturesque village nestled along the UNESCO-listed Geirangerfjord.
- Relax and take in the stunning views from your hotel or explore the charming village.

Day 6: Geirangerfjord Cruise
- Embark on a memorable Geirangerfjord cruise, surrounded by towering cliffs and cascading waterfalls.
- Experience the Seven Sisters Waterfall and the Suitor Waterfall, creating lasting memories for all.
- Opt for a guided kayak tour or a gentle hike to enjoy the area's natural beauty up close.

Day 7: Journey to Tromsø
- Fly from Geiranger to Tromsø, located in the Arctic region of Norway.
- Visit the Polaria Arctic Experience Center, a captivating place for the whole family to learn about Arctic wildlife and ecosystems.

Day 8: Arctic Adventures in Tromsø
- Take an exhilarating husky sledding tour through the Arctic wilderness, an unforgettable experience for all ages.

- Visit the Tromsø Ice Domes, a magical ice hotel with impressive ice sculptures.
- In the evening, go on a Northern Lights tour (in season) to witness the captivating celestial display.

Day 9: Return to Oslo
- Fly back to Oslo and spend the day exploring any missed attractions or enjoying souvenir shopping.
- Consider visiting the Norsk Folkemuseum, an open-air museum showcasing Norwegian history and culture.

Day 10: Departure from Norway
- Say farewell to Norway, departing from Oslo and carrying cherished memories of your multi-generational adventure.

This itinerary aims to balance exploration, relaxation, and interactive experiences suitable for every member of the family. From the dynamic city life of Oslo to the pristine beauty of Geirangerfjord and the Arctic wonders of Tromsø, Norway promises a remarkable journey that will be cherished by generations to come.

The Legend of the Northern Lights

Long ago, in the northern reaches of Norway, there lived a young girl named Ingrid. She was known for her kindness and a heart as pure as the untouched snow that covered the landscape. Ingrid lived with her family in a small village nestled between the towering mountains and the icy fjords.

One winter night, a mysterious traveler arrived in the village. He was a tall man with a cloak that shimmered like the stars in the night sky. The villagers gathered around him, eager to hear stories from far-off lands. The traveler, who called himself Nord, had an aura of ancient wisdom about him.

As the night wore on, Nord spoke of magical spirits that danced in the skies, painting the darkness with ribbons of color. He spoke of the elusive Northern Lights, a breathtaking phenomenon that few had witnessed. The villagers were captivated by his tales, and young Ingrid listened with wide eyes, her imagination ignited.

Ingrid was determined to witness the Northern Lights herself, and she asked Nord for guidance. The traveler smiled warmly at the young girl and told her that the spirits were elusive but could be summoned by those with pure hearts and unwavering belief.

The following evening, Ingrid ventured out into the frozen wilderness. The sky was clear, and the stars sparkled like diamonds. She stood atop a snow-covered hill and closed her eyes, focusing on her heart's deepest desire.

Ingrid began to sing a song, a song of love and hope, a song that came straight from her soul. Her voice soared into the night, and as she sang, the heavens seemed to respond. Swirls of green and purple light danced across the sky, weaving and twirling in mesmerizing patterns.

The Northern Lights had come alive before Ingrid's very eyes. She watched in awe as the celestial display filled the darkness with a magical glow. The lights seemed to whisper secrets of the universe, and Ingrid felt a profound connection to the world around her.

From that day forward, Ingrid became the village's Northern Lights guardian. She would sing her heart's song whenever the sky was clear, and the lights would appear, spreading joy and wonder among the villagers.

As years passed, Ingrid's legend spread far beyond her village, and people from distant lands came to witness the enchanting display she summoned. The Northern Lights became a symbol of Norway's beauty and mystery, captivating travelers from all corners of the world.

To this day, the legend of Ingrid, the girl who danced with the Northern Lights, lives on in the hearts of the Norwegian people. And on clear winter nights, when the sky is adorned with shimmering colors, locals and visitors alike remember the pure-hearted girl who gifted the world with the magic of the Northern Lights.

Printed in Great Britain
by Amazon